For my son, Louis

In memory of his grandfather Jean-Louis Festal
1947–2008

CONTENTS

If you have the desire for knowledge and the power to give it physical expression, go out and explore. If you are a brave man you will do nothing; if you are fearful you may do much, for none but cowards have need to prove their bravery. Some will tell you that you are mad, and nearly all will say, 'What is the use?'

Apsley Cherry-Garrard,
The Worst Journey in the World

PROLOGUE

Lacing Up

Christmas Day. The light from the west was sharp and watchful, a cusping breeze rose from the sea. It was not a long run, just far enough to feel myself moving at speed again. It had been over a week since I had last put on my trainers and already they had started to fold in on themselves. As I broke into motion I found it hard to believe that for most of the year I had been running up to 18 miles a day, and here I was, back at the beginning, wading through the sludge of an early afternoon run. One hour. Eight miles. That was all.

I ran my first marathon in London in 2000, but it was not until I had crossed the finish line in Paris six years later that I wondered what would happen if I kept going. That was where the question, why we run, first arose. Thirty thousand people had come to Paris to run through the city. Nearly 40,000 would be lining up later that month in London. For many it was an experience to be had once and only once. Thank you, but enough. For others, though, 26.2 miles is not enough, and when their legs have recovered, the search begins again to find a longer, harder challenge.

In *Nature*, Ralph Waldo Emerson wrote that 'Motion or change, and identity or rest, are the first and second secrets of nature.' In the end the question of why we run comes down to what happens when you head out on your Sunday-morning run, with your family asleep or making breakfast, and you keep going. Where does that road lead to? An increasing number of people know that it gets you at least as far as the marathon. And then there is a void. What happens after that?

I have no special knowledge, no privileged position. I have not won a single race in my life, nor can I run particularly quickly, but what I have learnt is that I have a capacity to run for a very long time without stopping. In itself this is no great skill – after all, no one is taught how to run – and long-distance running is an experience that can be shared by all. And yet what I have seen is something that few people have witnessed and even fewer have reported. If you want to know where that road leads, read on. If not, then you are already stronger, braver and more knowing than I ever thought I was capable of being.

Long-distance runners are, by their nature, solitary figures and to ask them why they run such epic distances is still usually met with the response that Chris Brasher, the founder of the London Marathon, got when he asked the same question: 'Come on, Chris, you know why.' Each runner has their own reason, in some cases their own cross to bear, and I have sat at the feet of those runners to learn from them, rather than to offer some kind of confessional on their behalf. Inevitably, though, motives have been uncovered and tragedies revealed. While these explanations alone do not give a three-dimensional picture of why they run, to ignore them would be to treat running as a pastime that exists mutually exclusively to the rest of their lives. For these men and women, as it came to be for me, running was as much a way of life as a means of understanding it.

My own confession is that I did not set out to write this story as a parable of my shift into adulthood, but as time went on that is what it became. I can only apologise if this upsets the rhythm of the story but I have learnt, belatedly, that this transition was intimately connected to the reasons why I run, and to avoid it would be to fail the narrator's primary obligation – honesty.

Some will be familiar with this journey, in its various guises, already. All who have put on a pair of trainers will know the sense of freedom that comes with fresh air on the face miles from home. What we come to feel in those moments of liberation is, as Emerson described it, like 'standing on the bare ground – my head bathed by the blithe air and uplifted into infinite space, – all mean egotism vanishes. I became a transparent eyeball;

I am nothing; I see all; the currents of the Universal Being circulate through me.' If you don't know this already, you soon will because, in the end, while I can show you where that road leads, to know, to really know, will require you to take to the road yourself.

As for the rest, they may never understand. They will look on with complete incomprehension at the idea of making life harder still, although they might listen politely before turning away. If you have told this story already, nearly all who listened will have thought that you were mad. They will almost certainly have asked: what is the use?

I

Orbiting

I had been running for about 4 hours by the time I dropped to my knees over a shallow puddle to contemplate breaking the muddy reflection and quenching my thirst. Around me the breeze rustled through the coarse heather that clung to the sandy soil, and from above came the occasional swoosh of the wind through the imperious evergreens that shaded me now from the summer sun. The landscape was in a state of deep meditative peacefulness, like a heartbeat at rest. My lips were chapped from dehydration, my tongue swollen and cumbersome. The crust of sweat that had formed on my biceps crackled to the touch and my shorts were starch-stiff, salt lines jagging across them like some terrible economic forecast. I was exhausted, confused and completely lost.

The road from which I had strayed in search of this muddy oasis opened up behind me, daring me to try to retrace my steps. How on earth had this happened? Earlier that morning I had pulled out the map and checked off ll the turnings of a 10-mile circular route that I remembered so clearly from a trip long ago. I had spent my summers growing up in this plantation forest of pine trees and heather, and there was even a family photograph taken of us kneeling down on a forest floor just like this. Moments later we had returned to our bicycles to ride back over the dunes and down the long winding road that led to the cottage by the sea. But the road I was on now could not possibly lead back to the sea because the noon sun overhead gave a clear indication that I was still heading approximately east, and away from my destination. However, even this observation could not be relied on to fix my geographical and temporal location since this was the west coast of Denmark at solstice when the sun behaves peculiarly, and for hours seemed to have barely moved across the sky.

It was the summer of 2002 and it had been four months since I had run my last marathon. Although I had started to waver, wondering how much longer I could keep going, the many miles I had run in training bolstered my confidence that I was going to be fine. I had not drunk anything since the cup of tea at breakfast, and even as I started pissing blood I had not become worried. It was not the first time this had happened, and as alarming as it was to discover that the kidneys had started to process themselves, I kept reminding myself – I am a runner. This is what I do. What was of greater concern was my growing emotional confusion. While the evidence of my physical limitations reinforced the fact that the body has the capacity to destroy itself from within, the moment that you start to choke with the longing to be home again is when your will to keep pushing on begins to falter. I wanted this to be over, and soon.

The road bears witness to all travellers who go on foot and each of us has a breaking point at which we have to recognise that we are no longer in complete control. Retracing my steps to this place was a way of savouring the memory of an era long past. However, it came with a warning. If I stayed too long, it would lead into the labyrinth of my childhood memories, which was scarcely a useful navigational tool. Kneeling down on the forest floor, I pined for home, and that homesickness was combined with a peculiar nostalgia that came from being confronted with a past I had not contemplated for a decade, made increasingly vivid the more fatigued and dehydrated I became. The longer I remained out on the road, the worse it would get.

As I rose to my feet, having talked myself out of disturbing my dark reflection in the puddle, all I was certain of was that 2 hours behind me was a railway line that bisected the main road back to the coastal village of Henne. Walking off the forest track and back onto the main road, I realised that my way home could be found in the place where landscape and memory collide. Through recollection, I could *think* myself out of this predicament, and the right path would emerge out of the silence. Against the shimmer of heat rising from the tarmac, I imagined myself getting back on my bicycle all those years ago. Turning my back to the wind, I made off in the direction I had no tangible proof was the direction of home.

Long before I was born, my parents had been coming to the west coast of Denmark as part of an annual trip to visit my maternal grandparents. Later, in a small cottage high on the dunes, my brother and I would pass a month of every summer running along the beach, flying kites against the North Sea wind. Every August, days before our departure from England, when the roads were empty of those who had already left for the long vacation, we would sit by the front door watching the inventory build up of clothes, towels, swimwear and cooking utensils. Bicycles would go onto the roof rack on the morning of our departure, and we would then, at last, be told to find a place in the back. As we drove through Essex to Harwich, with the fields already turning brown and dusty in the heat, our excited chatter would simmer to a patient anticipation. The overnight ferry took us to Esbjerg, where we waved to anonymous bystanders on the quay. The smell of diesel mixed with brine was the first sensory indication that we were finally, eleven long months later, returning to the coast.

The final mile of that two-day trip weaves gently

through the modest clapboard town of Henne, past ice-cream parlours from which the aroma of waffles and fish and chips carries on the breeze. The car, weighed down low to the ground like an amphibious vessel, rolled slowly past families lining up to play mini-golf. Huge German dogs padded obediently along the pavement, their owners silent and content with their modest holiday expectations as their children raced on ahead. In the months that had passed, little had changed. The innocence of the landscape and the simplicity of the routine that we quickly fell into meant that each time we returned it was as if we were doing so, apologetically, after a prolonged, unforeseen absence.

The road turned to gravel as it meandered lazily out of the other side of Henne, through the undulating plantations that we had known since our infancy, the cottage obscured from view until we were virtually on top of it. My father would bring the car almost to a standstill as he heightened the anticipation of our long-awaited arrival. And then it emerged, as if born out of the sand in front of us. The high, west-facing windows, covered in salt-water residue, and the battered roof were evidence of the years of howling gales and ferociously cold winters that we had never had to endure. Once again it was standing before us, gleaming in the sun.

Whole weeks would go by when my brother and I would vanish into the dunes to create entire universes that bore no relation to our normal everyday life. Our parents sat reading, unknotting kite-string or playing cards on the veranda, lifting their eyes sometimes to watch a fishing vessel sail into port. At the end of each day we would return to regale them with our stories as though we were adventurers returning from some undiscovered land. Every Saturday my brother and I raced into town to watch holidaymakers departing, their cars groaning under the weight of seafaring paraphernalia, and we would be thankful that we were not yet going back to England.

For my brother and me, the imaginary adventures we had had here brought this place to life. It was a transcendent attachment for both of us, yet completely genuine. When we were dragged to the car at the end of the month, blubbing that we didn't want to leave, we attempted to reason through our tears that we simply could not go home since this *was* home. Our childhood had taken root in the landscape, life here was as intrinsically bound to us as we were to it, and the pull that it had over us made even more bitter the knowledge that we would not be back for another year.

Runners are, by nature, domestic creatures, and there exists in all of us a gut instinct leading us back home. It was by no means the first time I had taken a wrong turning while out running, or followed a short cut into a dead end. But I had never endured anything like this before. It seemed as though I had lost the world, that if I lay down and closed my eyes no one would ever find me. And, when I later recalled that feeling of complete dislocation, I realised that until that day, even though I had run a couple of marathons, I had never questioned why I did what I did. To train and run a marathon is a mechanical action built out of hours of repetitive hard work. For years running, for me, meant little more than putting one foot down in front of the other. This experience of extreme physical and mental duress, on the other hand, was forcing me to question every assumption I had ever made about why we run such great distances at all.

No matter how great the attraction of the solitary hours spent on the road, home is the centrifugal epicentre of safety and belonging where each run begins and ends. In *Feet in the Clouds*, Richard Askwith's memoir of fell-running, he explicitly states that one of the greatest pleasures of running for hours across the fells is the warm bath and pint of beer that would be awaiting him on his return. Stop and reflect for a moment the next time you start to waver, and you will remember that getting back home lies at the heart of understanding one of the fundamental instincts of why we run. To a large degree we are unaware of it, and the instinct to return cannot be vocalised immediately. Most days we step onto the pavement knowing exactly how far we are going to run, the precise course, and we know too that we'll be back in time to shower before dinner. So long as we don't stray too far beyond what we know, we are sure that the call of home will not rise up, unromantically spoiling the occasion. We can then continue to nurture the feeling that we do really belong out here, temporarily estranged from the everyday – enjoying an adventure while life elsewhere continues with comforting predictability. The heightened awareness of this instinct arises only when we step, deliberately or not, beyond those boundaries of routine.

While I knew just what Askwith was talking about, it seemed that even when he was running for the best part of a day across the most hazardous terrain in Britain, part of his reason for doing so was specifically to manufacture a hyper-sensitised sense of longing. I was well aware of the pleasure we runners gain in rewarding ourselves for enduring voluntary suffering. However, it could be true only so long as the runner knows where he is going and is able to exert a level of control over his environment. So long as he stays within the limits of his ability, then this self-deception can be nurtured just enough to remain enjoyable.

The moment that we step into the discomfort zone, the longing for home begins to form without forewarning, like a sickness in the throat. In all the years that I had been running, I had never before experienced such a sense of dislocation, since I had always known where I was running, and home was just there, a permanent, almost forgotten, fixture in my journey there and back. My immediate reaction, as I stood dressed only in my T-shirt and shorts, was to sit down and have a good cry.

Homesickness has long been sentimentalised to the point at which the only legitimate sufferers were children away from their parents for the first time. Yet in 1688 Johannes Hofer observed that homesickness or nostalgia was a medical condition. The *nostos* of returning home, and the *algos* of pain or longing were understood as the pain a sick person feels because he wishes to return to his native land, and fears never to see it again. For Hofer, it was a condition that belonged to an era in which the great nations were perpetually at war and soldiers might spend years at a time in foreign lands, nurturing a very real belief that they might never again set foot in their native country. The debris of military campaigns is littered with individuals who were inexplicably close to death and were consequently sent home to die with their families. As soon as they came in sight of their city or country, they made a remarkable recovery, only to be returned immediately to the front line. Across a span of more than 300 years I understood exactly what Hofer meant. It was a vulnerability that manifested itself as a physical pain – a longing that comes out most forcefully in the language of a child.

Hofer considered it a serious condition whose symptoms were 'continued sadness . . . even palpitations of the heart, frequent sighs, also stupidity of the mind'. It was only by keeping the mind occupied and offering at least the hope of home that it could be cured. I became anxious only when I realised not simply that I had made a wrong turn, but that to turn back would mean pushing myself further than I had ever run before, and I was not sure whether I was up to it. Whenever I stopped to consider my options, my legs would begin to shake as much out of fatigue as fear of the distance still left to cover. And yet I knew, too deep inside me to compute logically, that all it would take was the glimpse of a familiar setting and my strength would be restored. The moment that happened, my faith in my own abilities would return and I would laugh off the blood and the tears.

As the world became smaller, and people moved more quickly across it, so Hofer's sense of pining became more defined. Homesickness became understood as a longing for a particular location, an idyllic place of tranquillity that often lay in the past. While the going had been good, confronting the landscape in which I had grown up and recalling the sweetness of those memories, it was as if I was actually running through my childhood. To survey the heather plantations and take in the salt-water breeze, which was just as I remembered it, made me feel as if I had never left. It was only the distance of years that prevented my reaching out and touching this charmed paradise just beyond my fingertips.

We had stayed up late the night before, listening to the waves crashing on the shore below. As I stumbled along the road, I tried to retrace my steps through the morning and into the previous night. How easy it was to recapture the smells and the drowsiness of that real joy, which was still only a few hours old! Before he disappeared under the waters of the Mediterranean, the pilot and author of *Le Petit Prince*, Antoine de Saint-Exupéry, recorded his life in the sky, writing that he felt most at home in 'a remoteness beyond possibility of homecoming'. While my body had been able to support me, I had slipped into a similar state of blissful, metronomic happiness. I felt as if I belonged here, delighting in a nostalgic self-deception. It was magical. And now that that had been lost, what I craved was the comfort of that simple memory. It was a homesickness for a place where I could still breathe deeply, where food would now be on the table, the door open to the summer breeze.

There was no single moment when I decided to become a long-distance runner. In those years when we ran barefoot across the sand, there was never any sense at all that I was born to run. Not yet a teenager, I was already too cumbersome to be capable of any great speed to consider that running was innate to my personality, and there were no great athletes in my family's past that suggested an appropriate genetic heritage.

The closest I could come to saying that running was in my blood was the knowledge that motion – or, more particularly, the desire to keep moving – has been the defining feature on both sides of my family as far back as I can trace. Even this was too obvious and heavy-handed a primary cause to explain why I kept returning to the road. Whilst they were not pioneers or mission-aries, when I plotted the settlement and upheaval of each generation of my family across the globe, it turned the atlas into an incoherent web of overlapping routes. On one side they head back and forth from England to New Zealand before coming to rest with my father in Oxford. On my mother's side, the path creeps up through *mittel* Europe just when the borders of the great nations were still in flux. Her family took root in Denmark for three generations before an abrupt divergence to Green-land and America, with my mother heading to England.

Three generations had been enough time for the family to make themselves at home at the heart of a small industrial town on the east coast of Jutland. Today though there is little evidence of the family that once was a proud source of industry. An unvisited gravestone marks the burial place of my grandparents, who were laid to rest on the same plot as my great-grandparents. I imagine that at one point they might have believed that theirs was a minor dynasty in the making and that they would be the venerated ancestors to whom their expanding number of offspring were forever indebted.

But the industry that paid for their burial site has long faded. The four of them now lie in an area of the town that is largely forgotten, between the railway station and the hospital. The plot is cared for by the cemetery keeper, paid to replace the flowers every month, as the last will decreed, even though it no longer has visitors. And the crane that once bore the family name, which used to heave coal off the ships arriving from Newcastle, is long since defunct and stands silently as the last remaining witness to a forgotten family history.

If you had passed me by in the plantation that day in the late summer of 2002, none of this would have been apparent. What you would have seen was that the hunger I had staved off had shrunk my stomach, drawing inwards the thin material of my running top, which stuck to my body with sweat. My mouth was wide open, as if trying to draw nutrition out of the air itself, and I was squinting against the glare of the sun since I had been foolish enough not to bring sunglasses with me.

What was going on deep within me, though, was far from obvious. The right side of my head was pounding with blood as dehydration worked its way into my brain. My shoes had started to squelch with sweat, my socks rubbing the skin that was loosening on the balls of my feet. Ordinarily we become aware of blisters only after the event as we examine the damage done, but here I could feel them slowly inflate with liquid, forcing me to alter the strike of my foot on the road until I felt them burst. After a brief moment of relief the skin would then fold, exposing the raw flesh, and another blister would form in its place. However, this pain paled into mild irritation compared to the rawness of my nipples, as they scratched against the material of my top and blood ran down my chest.

Whatever idea I had set out with in my mind that morning had been rapidly overtaken by my increased awareness of my overexposure to physical distress. Understanding the primary motivations that explain why we run would have to wait until I had stopped shaking my head at my own stupidity and the soles of my feet no longer burned with tenderness.

Running just two marathons had given me the arrogance to think that I could call myself a long-distance runner and that I knew all there was to know about the running experience. Not only did I consider that two marathons were enough to fortify me against the elements but, when pushed for an explanation for why I ran, I believed my own claim that it helped me escape the cavalry march of everyday life, as feeble as that sounded.

Running, to my mind, was little more than a way of getting away from it all, a feeling that is familiar to all of us. The runners I knew understood this emotional illiteracy and we did not have to explain ourselves to each other. When trying to articulate this feeling more fully to those who just didn't get the point of running at all, I could only offer a dumb sigh of indescribable happiness. I loved it. None of this came close, though, to describing the draw of the intoxicating freedom and self-empowerment that I would later discover to be at the heart of the richness of the running experience. In retrospect, I think it was precisely because that day, as I got lost amid the pine trees, I was overcome by a freedom I had never previously encountered – a feeling of not being hemmed in, for the first time in my life, by regulations or straight lines – that it took me so long to relearn the language that would sufficiently capture what it was to run. When I finally did get home I was so overawed by what I had been through that I got stuck on the idea that the runner's basic instinct was simply limited to heading out of the front door and returning an hour or two later. This, I would come to see, was only the beginning.

When I had recovered and returned to my sedentary life, I did not run again for several months, so humiliated was I by the whole episode. I did not want people to think that I was trying to pass myself off as a runner, and it was years before I told anyone what had happened. What I see now is that I was neither humble enough to fully appreciate the profundity of the running experience, nor sufficiently eloquent to explain, either to myself or to others, just why we run. More than anything else, that day I was shown the true vulnerability of the individual in the natural world, as my fundamental assumptions about my right to call myself a long-distance runner were destroyed. When I think back to that day I still shudder at my naivety. Perhaps, though, I would never have thought to question my assumptions at all, or my right to call myself a runner, if I had not been forced to confront head-on the fallacies that I carried with me every time I laced up a pair of trainers.

I was not alone in my failure. When the transcendental philosopher Henry Thoreau retreated to the woods to live, it was only in his later reflections on the choice he had made that he was able to articulate fully his decisive reasons for returning to nature. As he wrote in *Walden*, he returned 'to front only the essential facts of life, and see if I could not learn what it had to teach . . . I wanted to live deep and suck out all the marrow of life.' As eloquent an explanation as this is, the precision of his thoughts had not come until after the event.

Naive as I was in articulating these experiences of nature, they did explain part of the reason why I had almost always run alone and had never joined a running club. If running is a means of escaping the trials of everyday life, then it meant taking my life into my own hands. It meant running for myself. And, in part, that meant getting away from the jostling of others. Even when I had only just started running it was plain to see that its appeal lay in the simplicity of the action, taken

one step at a time, as well as in the possibility of noncon-
formity that it offered. We can run anywhere, anyhow
and at any time. Running should not be hemmed in by
schedules and routines. Its beauty derives from the fact
that it cannot be governed by the magnetic fields of
others. We run for ourselves.

It was only much later, when I came to reflect on the
path I had taken that day, when I had been reduced to
my bare essence, that I understood what Jean-Jacques
Rousseau had meant when he wrote, 'So now I am alone
in the world, with no brother, neighbour or friend, nor
any company left me but my own.' Early in his life
Rousseau had declared that humankind's natural state
was solitude, where man and woman would walk alone
through fertile forests, not speaking, and meeting only
long enough as was necessary for procreation. By
immersing himself in nature and turning his back on
other people, Rousseau was going in search of
humankind's original condition: one in which he was
'completely free' of society. As he contemplated his lot
on his tour of the filthy cobbled streets of Paris, he articulated his belief that the only time that we are free of
the dirt and the evil that men do to each other is in our
childhood, when the uncomplicated innocence of the
untilled landscape is mirrored in us.

When I had set off that morning, it was with the
understanding that for several hours I would be cut off
from all community and conversation. This is the choice

of the long-distance runner. If you are unwilling or unable to embrace that solitude – to turn your back on the steady course of your life as a social being – then you are ill equipped to take to the road for long distances at a time. But to strip down to one's simplest, most natural form as a being outside society, unadorned, unaugmented and solely dependent on one's own bodily strength, is to reveal oneself as both self-propelled and completely independent of other people. Through a total renunciation of the world, those hours of solitude amount to the only time when we become completely ourselves and are our own masters, with nothing to distract or hinder us. Rousseau described it as 'The only [time] when I can truly say that I am what nature meant me to be'.

These encouragements to self-empowerment are echoed by even the most amateur of long-distance runners. In those hours when we are cut off from telephone calls and the nagging reminders of our daily responsibilities, we enjoy an illusion of complete self-sufficiency in which we believe that we want for nothing. This experience of liberation comes not only from having left those responsibilities behind, but also from the belief that we have taken with us all that we require to sustain ourselves. For 4 hours or so, this dictum had been true for me. That morning, the physical capacity that I knew my legs had to keep me moving forward had given me the confidence to look at myself, dressed only in a pair of trainers and the flimsiest of clothes, and believe that the source of true contentment lay within me. I didn't need anyone else to achieve that.

It was in part to clear his mind of a working life that had turned against him that Andy McMenemy, one of the first ultra-marathon runners I came to know, decided to take on the 151-mile, six-day Marathon des Sables in southern Morocco. The heat hits 50 degrees, while the terrain is barren sand and wind-blasted rock that offers no shelter from the sun in moments of crisis. Many are incapacitated for weeks afterwards as the phys-ical machinery struggles to recover. Even for the best athletes it is a gruesome test, leaving the tissues rotting with fatigue. When a friend finished his first and only attempt, he flew back to England with great pride at his achievement, only to start coughing up blood. In a psycho-somatic reaction to what he had put himself through, his body took the final revenge as the capil-laries in his chest wall burst and he was rushed to hospital. When Andy first decided to run the Marathon des Sables he had never run a marathon before. Yet, as he prepared himself for the scorched earth, he understood that a week in the desert was a chance to burn off some of the bitterness towards those who had wronged him, as well as a chance to think more clearly.

He trained for eighteen months, carrying with him wherever he went the provisions he would need for a week in the desert. In the 45-degree heat he ran every step of the race and by the end had subsided into an

23

exhausted peacefulness that put his working week in context. By the time he crossed the finishing line he knew what he had to do to pick his life up again. He returned home empowered by having confronted what Rousseau saw as a natural state of self-reliance, and which Andy never realised he had, so entwined with and reliant upon other people had he become.

I knew from experience that without food or water the outer limits of my capacity lay at around 4 hours. The route I had calculated, had I followed it, would have got me home long before the time issue would even need considering. It is hard to recall exactly when I started to suspect that I was lost, and it was only when I began to feel the physical disintegration of my body that I recognised that I was heading into trouble. Each runner is different. For me it starts in my hips, with the joints starting to seize up. I could not resist the urge to touch them through the thin material of my shorts, as if it would help to keep them in place while I ran. It left an alarming feeling that it was just the synthetic material that was preventing their exposure to the elements. With gravity the seizure spread down through my legs and into the toes, several tonnes of pressure having already been pushed through my feet. Blisters continued to swell, detaching skin from flesh, before bursting again with every step. No matter how painful it gets, there is still something delicious about the awareness of one's physical presence that comes with this disintegration, as though it brings with it a heightened sense of self.

The mental unravelling is much slower to take hold and more debilitating. In the supreme confusion that racks the senses and the imagination, trains of thought become completely separated – thoughts fizz in the back of the brain like a light bulb about to pop. There comes too an urgency for what has been left undone before departure – shopping lists; unironed clothes; emails left unanswered. 'I must get back, I must get back' becomes a delirious mantra that we mumble to ourselves, all of which results in something like vertigo. It is only by putting one foot in front of the other that we keep ourselves from falling headlong into complete hysteria.

The first time I felt this fatigue was during my first London Marathon, which I had spent the minimum requirement of 100 days training for. Finishing in 3 hours 45 minutes, I had been too caught up in the carnival experience of being cheered on by tens of thousands of people to look too deeply into what it meant to run 26.2 miles. While I seized up in the final miles, reduced to snivelling in self-pity as the lactic acid flooding through my muscles brought my legs to a halt, there were friends waiting for me in the pub. Rather than savour the pleasure of the numbness as my body finally came to rest, as fast as I could I collected my medal and shuffled out of the finishers' enclosure because I could not wait to be greeted by them and boast about my heroics. In so doing I passed right over one of the greatest pleasures of long-distance running – relief that it was finally over.

The version of events that I came back with sparked horror in those who listened, most of whom had never met anyone who had run a marathon before. Over the weeks the story got better in the telling. As the suppleness returned to my legs so that I was able to descend a flight of stairs unaided and put on a pair of trousers without having to lie down, so the more natural an athlete I became. When, having finally recovered, I laced up my trainers a month later for a short run, I really did think that I had found something that I could excel at, since I had achieved with minimum effort something that others would never contemplate.

One marathon had made me believe that running long distances required nothing more than knowing how to put one foot in front of the other for 3, 4 hours or more. A childish enthusiasm had prevented me from seeing that the marathon is really a spectator sport, and a false scale against which to measure our true capacity. What long-distance running is truly about is measuring ourselves against a challenge that exceeds simple arithmetic, covering miles that we had not necessarily foreseen we would have to run. It is about knowing how to cope when the world turns against you.

★

The cottage in Denmark where we had spent our child-hood summers was a small, primitive, two-room hut run on cold water and without electricity. Every year, as we grew taller, my brother and I would fight over which length of the L-shaped sofa we would sleep on. At night we would be put to bed, listening to our parents whispering, the glass tinkling as they did the washing up. As we lay under the sloping eaves, our eyes were always drawn to a map behind a glass frame that could be seen properly only when lying down. The map depicted every shipwreck that had been recorded around the Danish coastline. Each one was marked on the fading paper with a black dot, and in the dim light of the paraffin lamp the parchment glowed a warm orange, full of imagined danger as it pointed the way to troves of lost treasure. On some nights, storms raged too hard for us to sleep and rain rushed in great whorls against the window like handfuls of gravel, making us jump. At such times we would draw the curtains and watch the miniature pinpoints of orange lanterns on the masts of the fishing vessels as they crossed the foreshortened horizon created by the huge waves. Sometimes minutes would go by before they re-emerged and one of us would point to the beacon, breathing out audibly in relief that they were safe, until they disappeared behind the next giant roll of water.

Throughout my childhood I was unable to go anywhere without my favourite book, *The Sagas of Erik the Viking*. Erik set sail into fantastical encounters with dragons and sea-monsters, but it was always to the chapter entitled 'At the Edge of the World' that I returned to read over and over again. On the way back from their adventures, their ship was dragged, by forces over which they had no control, to the waterfall that marked the very edge of the earth. Seemingly about to be cast into the infinite abyss, the crew accepted their fate. It was only Erik who had the presence of mind to cast the anchor back into the world, by which they scrambled to safety.

The story of his escape, through brilliance of mind as well as steely courage, gave me a sense of what was required of me if I was ever to find myself in a similarly tight spot. As Erik gave way to more profoundly real heroes, I began to wonder whether I too had the qualities that would win through in moments of adversity. As the adolescent birdcage of my chest rose and fell with anticipation of my own adventures, I wondered whether I too would have risked becoming one of those individuals defined by one moment, or whether I would, like the rest of the crew, resign myself to die on the edges of history.

The plantation forest on the west coast of Denmark would have been an unlikely place for such a story of triumph, but now, faced with the seemingly insurmountable prospect of getting myself out of this fix, my first instinct was not to grit my teeth — as all heroes in such moments do – but to try to hold back the tears that had started to cloud my vision. The sun had moved over, another couple of hours had passed, and I had little choice but to continue. Long gone was the invincibility that I thought my two marathons would arm me with every time I took to the road. Even the steady bounce that had kept my spirits lifted had withered away, as the sun foreshortened my shadow into that of a hunched, gnarled old man.

The main road that I was searching for bisects the railway track at the village of Hennestationsby. Even in my childhood it had been a thriving community with two bakeries, a post office and all the necessary attributes of a locus of activity. The smell of baking pastries that drifted out to the morning shoppers was the first sign that the moment of our summer arrival at the cottage was fast approaching.

There are hundreds of villages like this scattered the length of the country, all now fallen into whitewashed despair. The station guard house had been unused and locked for ten years, but the paint was always fresh, as if in anticipation of the line opening up again at any moment, allowing ordinary life to resume. Although all the children had left, nevertheless it was this forgotten corner of Denmark that seemed to me on that day a vision of paradise, since my arrival here would mean that my ordeal was nearly over.

Another hour passed as I concentrated on pushing

one leg down before bringing the other one up and forward and then waiting for gravity to play its part as I went through a laborious, slow-motion cycle of the running technique. Pain jagged up through my feet and into my knees before settling into my hips and spine as I used the force of my swinging arms to propel myself forward. There was no elegance or ergonomics left in me and I looked more like a prisoner dragging a ball and chain than the athlete I had set out as earlier that morning.

The first signs of life began to appear like spring leaves on a tree. A secluded nudist camp – a favourite of visiting Germans. I forced myself to lift my head from my chest and unfold my upper body from the peculiar foetal position that I had collapsed into while I ran. A road sign – a name I remembered – was like seeing a loved one appear out of a crowd on a station platform after a long journey. I felt a wash of excitement pouring into my brain at the prospect of someone rushing out to help carry my burden. The road had been turning imperceptibly and now that the sun was behind me I recognised this landscape. Around another bend in the road, the magical vision of Hennestationsby came into view. I was no longer lost! There were still 10 more miles to go, but I knew the incline and turn of every one of them. The needle of my internal compass was restored.

All runners feel a sense of pride when they return to the map plotting a recently covered route, their fingers travelling along roads, over fields and following paths that only those on foot can take. 'I did that. On my own.' No matter the distance covered or the time on the road, the pleasure of empowerment that comes with the accomplishment of a challenge is always profound and rewarding. When that day was finally over I learnt a little more about what it meant to be a long-distance runner. It takes that first time, when we get lost and become fully acquainted with our own vulnerability, for us to let go of those ties to home, and to better understand the illusory relationship between ourselves as autonomous individuals and our locus of sanctuary.

However, it was really only eight years later, when I met the people whose very existences were defined by running, that I came to see how profound a gap there was between the runner that I was and the athlete I thought I had already become. What I lacked more than anything else was the humility to appreciate how implacable the natural world can be when we cast ourselves into it with only a T-shirt, a pair of shorts and our trainers to protect ourselves. I could easily have gone the rest of my life without having confronted this truth. It is a reassessment that is easier to ignore and cannot be done all at once. But if you too decide to follow this route, you will discover soon enough that the first step comes when, intentionally or not, we are forced out of the orbit that draws us home.

★

The road passed by a garage. I stopped for several minutes on the opposite verge, contemplating how to get some water since I had no money on me. To the right of the petrol pumps was a car-washing service. A coiled-up hosepipe lay out of sight from the booth window where I could see that the cashier's back was turned towards me. As casually as I could, I crossed the road.

I could feel the water easing the pain in my throat even before I had turned the tap on. But when the water poured out it was sickly warm, the hose having lain in the sun all day. Letting it run, I kept glancing up at the booth and then, as I raised the hose again to my lips, the cashier came charging out, a fist raised comically above his head, yelling obscenities in German, then in Danish. I did not even have time to turn the tap off and a pool of warm water started to gather around me. I felt dizzy with surprise. I wanted to fall to my knees and beg him to let me drink, but I was already on the road again, being stared at in astonishment by a couple driving past, who had slowed down to watch the events unravel, jabbing their fingers at me in curiosity and accusation.

I could see now the blood running down my legs and arms from the chafing of my clothes, and I wondered what those who passed me by must have thought. When I had set out I had not been the only runner on the road, and, with my chin high and my arms relaxed by my side, I was an image of respectability and good health.

Now it looked as though I had been dragged out of a hurricane. There were family friends coming to visit. When their dark Mercedes swept past me, instantly recognisable as the car we had been forbidden to go near as children, I started to raise my hand to get their attention, but then remembered the proudly buffed leather seats. They would be faced with an awkward moral dilemma if they saw me. I dropped my arm.

As I turned the final corner, my feet barely scraping clear of the gravel, the pain and the desire for it all to be over became one. I had never longed for something so much. And now that I was confronted by the cottage, the rock upon which my longing to reach the end had been built, I felt let down that the sense of homecoming was not somehow replicated in my surroundings, as it had been when we were children. The cottage and the dunes on which it stood were as they had been when I had left that morning, the landscape magisterially in-different.

But there were my parents! They would have been worried sick, going through their own imagined journey as they became more and more anxious that some terrible tragedy had befallen me. I was five years old again, rushing to them from an afternoon of adventure, and the pain instantly evaporated. I half expected them to crash down the steps to greet me, to hold me close to them and make me promise that I would never do it again. I pulled myself up the final incline, feeling heroic as I tried to show both that I was in agony, but also that I was tough enough not to need the attention. I was the son returned from war whose manly chest was puffed out with courage and determination. With each step I was taking charge of the situation.

Except, of course, it was nothing like that. My father turned to look over his shoulder when he heard my final footfall, as if momentarily distracted. 'Hello, son.' And then he went into the house to fetch a tray of drinks. My absence had not been noted with any sense of alarm. I was a long-distance runner, after all — I was *meant* to go out running for hours at a time. That is what we did.

Even as I recounted the last hours to them it was plain to see that they were listening out of politeness. We were in the place of my childhood, not some foreign land. The adventures that took place here were the creations of an adolescent mind. To get lost was to concoct a fiction.

My thinly disguised disappointment at the casual reception I received on my return was due entirely to my failure to acknowledge one of the most basic truths about what it is to leave home and take to the road. Home, for the runner, is always a gravitational point to which our internal compass points, especially in moments of danger or distress. The further we run and the greater our sense of longing, the more emotionally charged our vision of that locus of safety becomes, until eventually we start to expect that it will reflect perfectly our precise inner emotional state. 'As within, so without,' as the Greek poet Hermesianax wrote.

But this is not possible since the very otherness of the landscape, of people, of home, makes others merely mute witnesses, entirely reliant on our account of events for any emotional understanding. To know what it is like to fall apart on a run would require them to go out there and do it themselves. No amount of storytelling can accurately portray that experience.

The dominant place of home in our daily lives means that, until we have stepped outside its reach, it has a pull over us that will always make us return, and until we have learnt the position of home in our lives as runners, it will always control our every step. To become true long-distance runners, we must accept that we are completely on our own. Only once we have unshackled ourselves from that place of safety can we say that out there, in whatever state we end up, is where we belong.

In the years that have passed since that day it has taken the many thousands of miles I have covered for me to be able to defend myself sufficiently against the urge to return home, as well as to be able to articulate this fully. Now that I know how it feels, and now that I can give it a name, I can control it. For that I am a better, more

mature runner, able to see the signs of the first disintegration and combat it appropriately.

And yet, I am quite willing to admit that I still often
fail myself: a bus ride home seeming like a more sensible
end to a run; the last few miles discarded in the logic
that I have run far enough. Underneath that weakness
for the easy way out I have come to see that, until we
have detached ourselves fully from the notion of home,
the unfettered freedom of the road will always be limited
to an illusion. Whether in Denmark, in Athens or on
the peaks above Lake Windermere, for as long as I was
still attached to some thread of elastic that stretched and
then contracted, reeling me in towards home, I would
always be constraining my own capacity and cutting
myself off from the ultimate possibilities that running
offers.

After the escapade in Denmark I ran a marathon
almost every year, fortified by the memory of that experience. None of them measured up to that day's revela-
tions. My times got better; I learnt more each year about
how to pace myself, as well as recognising the importance of preparation and months of long weekend runs.
It is no coincidence, however, that the year I turned
from someone who ran marathons into a true long-
distance runner was also the year that I forced myself
to take on a different routine in my training.

Instead of stepping onto the pavement for a loop of
an hour to return to my front door 8 miles later, I would

buy a train ticket upstream through the Thames Valley to Hampton Court and run the 20-mile length of the river back home. There were no short cuts, no easy ways out when those leaden moments of despondency descended. All I could do was follow the crooked line of the river. Not only did it force upon me an obligation to continue, but it also heightened that sense of return to a single definable point. I was able to make a clear distinction between myself and home, even if I could not shake off the delicious awareness that in 20 miles' time I would be rewarded with the warmth of a hot bath and a pint of beer. The rest of the afternoon would then be spent sitting numb and half asleep in front of the television with a slightly moronic smile on my face in the knowledge that I had finished another 100 miles for the week. The difference now was that by setting myself far enough out of its immediate gravitational pull, I was able to control the status of home in my life as a runner.

Falling into the sentimental trap of self-congratulation, I later worked out that I had run 35 miles that summer's day in Denmark. It was the first time that I had experienced the freedom that Andy McMenemy would describe some years later as blowing out the taint of the everyday, in abandonment and solitude. That experience, at its full capacity, has the ability to bring us home like a stranger from a distant land, flushed with glory and stories of exploits, which exhilarates until it inevitably fades. And when it has faded, that is the time to put on the trainers again.

In the middle of winter, especially, we all know how hard it is to turn our backs on the warmth of the living room. And then we remember the adventures and rewards that await us. Having conquered the sometimes overwhelming urge to give up, then any distance, any amount of time on our feet becomes conceivable. I know now that it is only in these precious hours, out in the theatre of the wild and in our own discomfort zone, far away from the distraction of family and friends, that we can truly enjoy what running has to offer. When that moment of realisation comes, perhaps when you are lying in bed on a Sunday morning waiting to get up, it will consume you. It will manifest itself as an itch, a physical lusting after the moment when you can put on your trainers and be on the other side of your four walls. At that moment, 'out there' ceases to be a place of trepidation and fear, and is transformed into a place where we feel most alive, most uninhibited, most ourselves. Until then, there will always be a moment when that longing for home arrives, pale and sickly in a lapse of concentration, difficult to ignore and impossible to shake. To become a true long-distance runner, our first duty to ourselves is to negate that longing absolutely.

2

First Steps

There is a road west out of Cheltenham that narrows and rises quickly to a rocky footpath as it follows the gradient up Sandy Hill. Before the path leads back down the supersonically steep pastures of Daisy Bank, through which we had slid on our knees as schoolchildren, there is a point where the gradient levels off. Here footpaths have been worn erratically into the hilltop, linking the different panoramic views as if wanderers arriving here for the first time are so spoilt for choice that they don't know where to gaze first. It had been fifteen years since I had last been here, and I had read enough James Ellroy novels to know that before I looked to the future, to the place where my journey as a runner was going to take me, I would first have to solve the riddle of cause and uncover the reasons why I had become a runner at all.

After I had checked in, I slipped down the hotel fire escape to avoid startling the gentrified clientele. The September light was fresh, and the watery air told of the staleness of a summer that had finally been washed out. I scrambled up the hill towards the rapidly setting sun, paused for a moment by a bench covered in moss and looked out at the lush green basin beneath me. The temperature was dropping and I would have to get down off the hill before it got dark.

As schoolchildren we had run here at least once a week, and the last time had been just after my A-level exams. That afternoon all the whistles from the sports fields had gone quiet and there had been no more games for us to play. We were just marking time before we could move on with our lives. I had come up here as much out of boredom as to watch the last days of our lives as children being acted out. On my return I found a sadness, which previously I was only dimly aware of, that had petrified in my liver over the years. For a moment it felt as if I were revisiting a crime scene, searching for clues as to where I had taken a wrong turn, unable to find my way back.

Through those difficult years of adolescence it had been the corridors of convention, circumscribed first by my parents and later by my school, that had shaped who I was. I had arrived, aged fourteen, to start a new school, my shoes rubbed clean, my nylon shirts in the wardrobe that would never need ironing. I surrendered immediately to the boundaries that were set down, glad of perimeters so clearly demarcated within which I could wander safely. It meant that I could concentrate on finding a place for myself within the system. Until I had learnt to think for myself, which did not happen until much later, I was happy to follow instructions, to obey orders and, for the most part, to stay within the white lines that marked the borders of moral conduct laid down for us. In this enclosed environment, where we were protected as much from ourselves as from the outside world, all danger was neutralised. While, perhaps, there was no explicit intention of neutering our personalities, any erratic behaviour that we had arrived with was quickly taken care of. By the time they had finished with us, we would be well on our way down the corridors that led to the lives our parents had.

The forced march down these corridors meant that any real adventures only ever happened in the hot summer days when we would disappear for months into the long grass of puberty. Those adventures came more easily to others. With the start of each new school year, friends returned to the school gates full of stories of conquests that were recounted for weeks as our tans faded. Their romances seemed like those hidden in the shadows of the coming-of-age novels I had read and, in their repetition, made my own. Every September we returned, our hair grown long, our voices a little deeper, and we pretended that we were closer to becoming adults. But the white lines were soon boxing us back in, and after a while even those who had grown up most were contained again within the routine of the classroom, our imaginations suffocated by the steady progress that was meant to lead us, with a greater store of knowledge, into adulthood.

The white lines even followed us onto the sports field, and each afternoon we would step onto the grass dressed in regulation shorts and trainers, knees now pink in the autumn breeze, and wait for our names to be called out. It was here that the physicality of adolescence was most keenly displayed. Our hormones became charged like electrons as we ran around, crashing into each other like some peculiar demonstration of particles in flight according to Brownian motion, which we had learnt about in physics over in D Block.

It was here too that I watched my own body grow thick and heavy, forcing me to negotiate my changing centre of gravity. I had once been good at these sports, but with each passing summer I seemed to leak a little more co-ordination, and the simple act of moving in a straight line became inexplicably complicated. I had now grown tall enough to be noticed, but my height had no strength, and there was no substance to my flesh. It was as if I had been cooked from the inside out and I had yet to gain any purchase on my muscles. I was not the only one. Each autumn our collective number grew, and for weeks we would not be allowed near a ball, so lacking in talent had we become. On the adjoining pitches the senior teams stripped off and played at being adults, passing the ball from one to another in studied concentration. When the whistle blew we filed out of the gates for another run up Sandy Lane. If our meagre aptitude was lost on the opposite team, we could at least offer some resistance by being fit enough to 'run them off the park', as we were told by way of encouragement.

When I reached seventeen, the issue of my vertical growth had ceased to simply affect my co-ordination and for a year, on the doctor's instructions, I stopped taking part in team sports altogether. While an unfathomable distance seemed to have opened up between me and my feet, pain speared my back where my spine had grown too quickly for the muscles to support it and warned of pressing the vertebrae out of shape. There were days when the pain left me prostrate on the hard changing-room floor, the only place I felt comfortable, looking like the tortured victim of some human sacrifice.

When I finally began to take part again, I tried to keep up on the pitch but soon slowed to a halt. Instead, I took to walking and then slowly running again up the crumbling path of Sandy Lane. As I regained my composure, my strength slowly catching up with the rest of me, I took to running up those steep paths long after the bell for dinner had rung. I would return to the school dining room to eat alone, the last of the chatter echoing from the hall doorway. I remember no great exhilaration or epiphany that came as I ate cold remains, and the lights were turned off around me. I was just happy that I could move freely once more.

Oscar Wilde, in his *De Profundis*, commented on the Greeks' recognition that there was a beauty in motion. I found that concept difficult to capture in words as I conquered another length of Sandy Lane. For Wilde it seemed that 'we all look at Nature too much, and live with her too little'. The Greeks, he wrote, 'saw that the sea was for the swimmer, and the sand for the feet of the runner'. They understood that running was a primeval action so uncomplicated that it should be celebrated for its purity. It provided a chance to be in concert with nature, offering an experience that was open to all.

At the end of our final term we took part in the last sporting tradition before going our separate ways for the holidays and were bussed out of the school gates for the annual cross-country race. For most it was an event so underwhelming, with the arousals of summer beckoning, that they came loaded with more cigarettes than they could possibly hope to smoke in a single afternoon. We started high up on Leckhampton Hill, stringing together the miles as we cut and turned across the open fields before starting down Daisy Bank.

In that final descent, the sweat streaked across my face like rain moving horizontally across a plane window at take-off. I hurtled downwards, the wind screaming in my ears, my mouth bursting open in exhilaration as I tried to catch my breath. Even as the ground flattened out beneath me, my legs kept moving faster and faster. I could not compute the speed at which I was travelling as I overtook one, two and then nine, ten people. It was as if all the energy that I had not engaged in the last year had erupted all at once, and I could not speak for amazement at how it felt. When I finished, fourth, all I could think of was wanting to go and do it all over again. Our sports instructor was so surprised to see me at the finishing line that he had to ask my name for the records.

It was in a similar moment of reckless inhibition, while playing alone on the beach, that Roger Bannister unearthed the beauty of running. 'I glanced around uneasily to see if anyone was watching. A few more steps – self-consciously . . . the earth seemed almost to move with me. I was running now, and a fresh rhythm entered my body.' Stumbling, as if quite by accident, upon the revelation, Bannister became 'both startled and frightened' as he discovered the power that resided in his legs. As a schoolboy he had been told that if he carried on running he would be dead by twenty-one, but he had fallen in love with the notion that there was an energy lying deep within his body that could be released simply by putting one foot in front of the other. Although it took him some years to work out what to do with his unquantifiable strength, from that moment on he never felt more alive than when running.

When Bannister's team arrived in Helsinki for the 1952 Olympics he was still a full-time medical student at St Mary's Hospital and had yet to finish his PhD. But he was sufficiently well known that people came to watch him train. At 6 feet 1 inch, 'with a chest like an engine block', he was the very picture of economy as his legs moved as easily as milk pouring from a jug, his arms pistoning back and forth. It was said that he did not run, but flowed around the track.

In the early 1950s British athletics was at a crossroads. Before the Olympics had been revived in the late nineteenth century, athletic endeavour in Britain was primarily restricted to inter-university races and pedestrianism. Even as athletics had become more grounded in science – with beer replaced by water, four-course meals discarded in favour of restrictive diets – Bannister had repeatedly said that, for him, athletics was just another dimension to his already busy life. He would not let training upset the balance of his week. When he found out that he would have to race twice before reaching the 1,500-metre finals, he knew that his half-hour training sessions four times a week were not going to be enough. The Games were a disaster and he trailed in fourth place. As Britain's greatest hope on the track he became the lightning conductor for the dark skies of criticism that the team received when they arrived back in London.

At the turn of the twentieth century, the mile was

considered the pinnacle of athletic endeavour. The 100 metres was about speed, the marathon about endurance, but the mile required a perfect combination of both, and as the century progressed so too did the quest to break the 4-minute barrier. Until the late 1930s many still considered it impossible, citing the fact that even the great 'flying Finn', Paavo Nurmi, had missed it – albeit by only 10.4 seconds in 1924. In 1935 the brilliant track coach Brutus Hamilton wrote an article for *Amateur Athletics* magazine, based on rigorous scientific research and data on human structural limits compiled by Finnish mathematicians, in which he stated that the fastest a human could run a mile was 4:01.06. As well as its being a natural barrier to aim for, trainers saw that there was also a mathematical elegance to the 4-minute mile that made it an enticing proposition. As one writer explained, the figure 'seemed so perfectly rounded – four laps, four quarter miles, four point-oh-oh minutes – that it seemed God himself had established it as man's limit'. Added to which it was the ultimate individual event. There was no place to hide behind team-mates or a slow field: it was one man's race against the clock.

Four years would be too long for Bannister to wait to seek his revenge at the next Olympics, and in the months that followed his return to Britain he started to talk openly about his assault on the mythical record. In 1953, as Edmund Hillary prepared for the greatest ever expedition to Everest, Bannister sat down to work out how to decode the most celebrated enigma in athletics.

After much persuasion, Bannister agreed to take on a coach, realising from his failure at Helsinki that he could not succeed on his own. But he was still not prepared to sacrifice every other area of his life for athletic greatness. Down to the laces of his running shoes, he was one of the last generation of Victorians who had been brought up amongst the Greek ideals that athletic pursuit was essential to the healthy life – *mens sana in corpore sano* (a sound mind in a sound body).

While few who take to the road after a long day in the office harbour the dream of attempting, let alone running, a 4-minute mile, it is this spirit of Bannister's that we have inherited. Not many of us would entertain for long the idea of giving up everything else just to run. Even the challenge of training for a marathon is framed in the understanding that it is a means to an end, rather than an end in itself. Putting aside the motivation of raising money for charity, which lures so many to take part, what we seek in running is the enrichment that comes with every hard mile covered. We run to bring depth to our everyday lives, not the other way around.

Bannister vowed to continue his rounds of the wards at St Mary's Hospital and he would still travel up to Oxford once a week to deliver his tutorial papers. He wanted to show both his critics and his admirers that the 4-minute mile could be achieved without total sacrifice.

And how the British public clamoured for his success alongside the conquest of Everest on 29 May 1953 and the Coronation of Queen Elizabeth that had taken place on 2 June as Hillary had made his way down to base camp. Once Bannister announced his intentions, the papers had a full year to formulate their headlines, and they did not disappoint. When Bannister crashed through the tape on 6 May 1954 in 3:59.40, it was an event that 'put Great Britain back on top of the sporting world again'. 'The Empire was saved,' they declared. 'The impossible was no longer out of reach.'

When the cameras stopped rolling, Bannister returned to the wards at St Mary's Hospital as quickly as he could, but with a contentment that was more profound than his enjoyment of a busy, healthy life. Bannister had grown up in the last days of the empire, whose final years, set against the backdrop of war, had been shaped by explorers staking a claim to the last unconquered parts of the earth. These great British eccentrics, who had cast off into the unknown without fanfare, had been deified when they came to grief through their curiosity and the fallibility of their judgement. Bannister too saw himself as an explorer, challenging the boundaries that had long been thought inflexible, edging closer to an ideal that had been talked about for more than fifty years, an impulse that makes some people keep going when all others have turned back and push themselves to the very perimeter of human capacity.

By the early twentieth century the British public were taking an increasing interest in the discoveries of both pure and applied science, whose technological developments indicated a future of incomparable prosperity. Meanwhile, the reports from those returning from the four corners of the globe seemed to promise that it would soon be mapped out and conquered, making it accessible to all. The stories and the specimens brought back by explorers such as those on the 1874 Challenge Expedition, which had spent three weeks researching within the Antarctic Circle, aroused great curiosity at home while feeding a growing appetite for adventure. For these Victorian explorers, seeking out the remotest outposts of the planet was, above all, an intellectual pursuit. Those who journeyed into the unknown knew that they were sacrificing great professional futures by abandoning their careers in pursuit of knowledge and danger on frozen plateaus 12,000 miles away.

Fritjof Nansen, the first and greatest pioneer of polar travel, summarised in few words the tradition that had enveloped him: 'The history of the human race is a continual struggle from darkness towards light.' It was this sentiment that most precisely summed up the motivation of these explorers. For Apsley Cherry-Garrard, one of the youngest members of Scott's 1911 Antarctica team,

the notion of discovery for the sake of mapping the
unknown could be traced back to at least James Cook's
Southern Expedition of 1772 in the *Resolution* and the
Adventure, which had 'laid the foundation of our knowledge'. Cook's ships had been sent forth in the combined
spirit of state aggrandisement and individual striving, but
by the latter half of the eighteenth century the British
public had come to see scientific learning – the struggle
towards the light – as a motive in itself.

Cherry, as he was affectionately known, was a last-
minute addition to Scott's party and travelled as an
assistant zoologist, his scholarship and extreme short-
sightedness initially making his value intellectual rather
than physical. But he was in good company, as the team
were intent on stepping off the map and going beyond
the boundaries of what was known about polar exploration for the sake of knowledge itself, rather than out
of some misplaced display of masculinity. Cherry knew
from Scott's previous expedition, of 1901–4 that Scott
was too genuinely interested in the science of Antarctica to see it primarily as a journey for the glorifica-
tion of the empire, even when he received Amundsen's
one-line telegram from Madeira: 'BEG LEAVE TO INFORM
YOU FRAM PROCEEDING ANTARCTIC. AMUNDSEN.' (Fram
was Amundsen's ship.) As Cherry committed to his
diary, Scott was, above all, out 'for everything we could
add to the world's store of knowledge about the
Antarctic', and his only real ambition extended to 'not

only [going] farther than anyone had been before, but *as far as it was possible for man to go* [italics added]'.

From the day that Cherry left his family estate in Hertfordshire to meet Scott for the first time, he understood that for Scott 'exploration is the physical expression of the intellectual passion'. The Antarctic represented the unknown and for that reason alone demanded to be investigated throughly, in spite of the risks, and not for any commercial or vainglorious reasons. Even the ship in which they would set sail on 1 June 1910, *Terra Nova*, for the best scientifically equipped voyage south, was a homage to that very British intellectual pursuit.

In public, however, the personal motivations had to be made palatable for a nation full of self-doubt. 'The main object of this expedition', Scott wrote in a public appeal for the £40,000 needed, 'is to reach the South Pole, and secure for The British Empire the honour of this achievement.' The majority of the team shared Scott's private sentiment, though they were crushed to find that Amundsen, in refusing to allow science to get in the way of the business of getting to the Pole first, had beaten them by a month.

When Cherry, who had not been selected for the team's final assault on the South Pole, heard that the crowds had assembled to mourn the deaths of Scott, Oates, Wilson, Bower and Evans, following the failure of the expedition less than a year after the sinking of the *Titanic*, he realised that the public needed some kind

of reassurance. For the British people, while the clouds
of the First World War were slowly gathering and the
tide of the empire was in full retreat, all of which fostered
a climate of self-questioning, it would take time to
comprehend Scott's deeper motives. They needed to adopt
the martyrs as heroes, not out of some imperialist
triumphalism, but quite the reverse. The expedition was
a confirmation 'that the moral qualities that had once
made [their country] great were still intact'.

When he returned from the dark, his teeth shattered
from the intense cold, the bodies of Scott, Wilson, Bower
and Evans recovered and buried in the ice, Cherry volun-
teered for the First World War. Although he was invalided
out with chronic colitis, once home he did not write
of the horrors of the trenches, saying that the bravery
and the ideals of any soldier he had seen in combat
could not compare with those of the Antarctic explorers.
Instead, he endured numerous nervous breakdowns to
piece together the psychological landscape of the places,
'as far as it was possible for man to go', that these men
– who had not wished for public applause and were
now eternally embalmed in the ice, at the furthest
extremity of the earth – had gone to map.

'It is a pleasing picture to look back upon now,' he
opined from the warmth of his own fireside as he put
together the pages that would become *The Worst Journey
in the World*, but what repeatedly broke Cherry in the
recollection was the inability to relieve himself of 'such

extremities of suffering [that] cannot be measured'. He believed that it was not conventional heroism that had kept Scott's team going when the ponies had failed them and the rations had dwindled to nothing, for that would have been merely 'a display of foolishness'. For Cherry, the truly brave, amongst whom he numbered Scott, are made of 'fear and faint-heartedness'.

Cherry compared Scott to his friend T. E. Lawrence, of whom he wrote that 'the fact that in the eyes of the world Lawrence lived the bravest of lives did not help him prove to himself that he was no coward'. For most of us are cowards, and had Lawrence not been one too, he would have had no need to prove his bravery, because 'the man who is not afraid has no feelings, no sensitiveness, no nerves; in fact he is a fool'. Like Lawrence, Scott was extremely sensitive to his own limitations and did all he could to overcome them. It was this ability that made him stand out, since the lust for knowledge and exploration was much more a matter of mind than of body, a psychologically fuelled ambition more than a physical challenge.

Cherry had seen with his own eyes that it was the 'sensitive men', 'the men with nerves', who 'went furthest, pulled hardest and stayed longest'. They were not athletes who had trained for months while 'sleeping a good nine hours a night, eating carefully regulated meals and doing an allotted task each day under scientific control'. For weeks they had 'turned in at midnight to take off [their] clothes, eating when they could'. And yet, they were the ones who came through. These twelve adventurers, chosen from 8,000 applicants, had understood that theirs was a journey as much to the limits of their mental capacity as to the outer regions of any icy wasteland.

It is no coincidence that Cherry had been close friends at Winchester College with George Mallory, the most famous climber lost on Everest, who shared Cherry's idealism. He disappeared on his final ascent to the summit on 8 June 1924. In Mallory, Cherry saw a man 'burning with a kind of fire, an ardent impatient soul, winding himself up to a passion the higher he got'. It was this love of the unknown, this desire to walk off the map and see what was there, that consumed them both. It was the tradition Hillary carried with him in the conquest of Everest in 1953. This was literally so on his trans-Antarctic Expedition in 1957–8 when he took with him a copy of Cherry's history as a guide to 'the most spectacular discovery of an historical nature to be made in the Antarctic for many years'.

Sir Francis Younghusband, a veteran of the early assaults on Everest who had climbed with Mallory, knew well what kind of man was prepared to take himself to the very limits of human possibility. He spent the weeks while acclimatising at base camp writing in his diary, explaining why the expedition was there. After all, 'there is not the slightest sign of any material gain whatsoever – not an ounce of gold, or iron, or coal, or a single precious stone, or any land upon which food or material could be grown. What then is the good of it all?' It was, of course, a rhetorical question, and he answered it in a way that Cherry, Scott and all who, like Hillary, came later, would understand. 'The most obvious good is an increased knowledge of our own capacities. By trying with all our might and with all our mind to climb the highest point on earth, we are getting to know better what we can really do . . . if . . . we can reach the summit, we shall know that we are capable of more than we had supposed.'

Mallory too wrote of his own compulsion, compressing his burning ambition to climb Everest into a single line to his wife: 'I can't tell you how it possesses me.'

Even as long ago as those schooldays this, in my own small way, was what running represented to me. Running outdoors is to be in a sort of magical kingdom under whose spell I feel happiest. What matters more than anything else is seeking out the challenge of the distance and the terrain, throwing all my effort and daring into conquering it. What is revealed each time in taking on that challenge is a world of light and beauty, offering a temporary escape from the human condition. It is the closest thing we, as runners, can get to replicating the explorer's step into the unknown. In those hours spent alone, my legs heaving, sweat dripping from my forehead, my lungs feeling as though they are being torn apart, nothing else matters. There is no need to invent further justification. There is just the thrill of mapping out my own topology through the landscape, coming to know a little more about my own ability.

No matter how many of us are on the start line, or even that there is a start line, the lure of running great distances is always primarily a deeply personal one, anchored in the possibility of testing our own mental and physical capacities against the wasteland we run through. There is never any other value to it than what we give it. Of course, there is never any sense that I am playing on the frontiers of life and death, but in running I had found, without at first knowing it, a taste of the freedom that Scott, Cherry and Mallory had sought.

For those who attempted Everest, first in 1922, then again in 1923 and 1924, what had started out as a great Victorian adventure became something of a pilgrimage, a spiritual journey into the unknown. But in the end, even they knew, as Cherry had known, that their efforts were futile. 'If you have the desire for knowledge and the power to give it physical expression, go out and explore. If you are a brave man you will do nothing: if you are fearful you may do much, for none but cowards have to prove their bravery. Some will tell you that you are mad, and nearly all will say, "What is the use?"' In his brilliant mountaineering memoir, the pioneer Lionel Terray did not wait 600 pages before confessing that exploration was much more about discovering the boundaries of one's own limitations than leaving a tangible legacy. He simply entitled the account of his life's work *Conquistadors of the Useless*.

There is no such thing as a 'good death', except in the theological sense, only a life lived out bravely and authentically to the end. Scott had achieved that; Mallory and Terray too, who fell to his death in 1965, his memoir a prophetic *mea culpa*. For none was death an escape. Mallory would have kept returning to Everest until he had finished what he had started, but he would not have wanted to die there. The public sought some good in these explorers' last expeditions in an attempt to rescue something that would counterbalance the futility of their deaths. The greatest gift these men gave us was a profound ability to communicate the experiences of human nature at the limits of its endurance. The failures and deaths of these explorers, in whose footsteps we unavoidably tread, are transcended by their having articulated what is humanly possible. Today, in a world that has been almost completely mapped out, few of us can hope to emulate that bravery and sheer bloody-mindedness, although we can aspire to live out our lives more authentically. This is why the words that Cherry carved on the wooden cross on Observation Hill by their base camp in Antarctica, set high above the barrier on which Scott's frozen body still lies – 'To strive, to seek, to find and not to yield', from Tennyson's 'Ulysses' – are meant for us too.

★

'You want to run *how* far?'

I have no recollection of where I first heard of the Spartathlon, but the idea of running 152 miles non-stop from Athens to Sparta in under 36 hours came one Sunday morning in what anthropologists call any atypical finding in their field: 'an isolated occurrence'.

Eight years had passed since I had taken part in my first marathon and though I had run several since there was nothing on my resumé that suggested I had any right to take on what was described as the toughest footrace on earth. In those eight years, the challenge of running the marathon had transformed from being a test against the distance – could I succeed at all? – to a much more personal one – could I beat my last time? As hard as I trained, no matter how much more ergonomic I became in my action, it made little difference, since I simply could not get around any faster than 3 hours 30 minutes. By the time I had discovered the Spartathlon, some of the magic of running 26.2 miles had started to fade. Consciously or not, I knew it was time to start looking for another challenge.

If there was any logic to the decision, then it came in the question I had asked myself when I crossed the finish line in Paris two years previously. I had trained harder than ever before and, for the first time, had felt no crushing pains, as happens when the legs seize up with lactic acid. Taking off my medal, frustrated that I had come within

36 seconds of breaking the 3 hours 30 minutes barrier, I idly wondered how much further I could have run. Five or 10 miles? Could I have done it all over again?

RAF Wing Commander John Foden was confronted by a similar need for perspective when, in 1978, nearing his fiftieth birthday, he completed his first marathon. When he crossed the line he realised that he had no idea how the marathon had originated. In 490 BC, he read, Darius, the ruler of Persia, the mightiest empire the world had then seen, sent an army of 25,000 men west to conquer Greece and bring Athens under his control. Conquering the Ionian Islands and Eretria by midsummer, the Persians regrouped and sailed for Attica, 'flushed with victory and confident that they would treat Athens the same way'. In early August they landed in Marathon.

Herodotus' *Histories* provides the most contemporary account of the deeds of Pheidippides, a foot messenger who was sent to run the 152 miles from Athens to Sparta to enlist Spartan support against the invading Persians. While his recounting of some events is less than reliable, according to the *Histories* Pheidippides arrived some time 'the next day' to find the Spartans mid-festival and unwilling to help. By the time Pheidippides had run back to the generals at Marathon with the news from Sparta that they would not fight, he had covered over 300 miles.

The victory over the Persians was decisive, a defining

moment in Western history, according to John Stuart
Mill. Five hundred years later, in the self-apparent celebration of Athenian democracy, *On the Glory of Athens*,
Plutarch tells of a messenger called either Thersippus or
Eukle who returns from Marathon on foot with the
words, 'Rejoice, we conquer!' In his last poetic act he
was immortalised by promptly collapsing and dying. A
century later, in the hands of the satirist Lucian of
Samosata, the messenger's name had been changed to
Philippides. Pheidippides' epic, but not unique, feat for
a professional messenger was then conflated with the
symbolism of the victory of the emerging democracy.
When Robert Browning had finished with him in his
1879 poem celebrating the Athenian hero, the myth had
been updated and Pheidippides had been handed a sword
to help slay the Persian army.

Bothered that no one knew whether Pheidippides'
journey could actually be done, in 1980 Foden arrived
in Greece, equipped with nothing more than pages from
the *Encyclopaedia Britannica* and some athletics magazines
that contained advice on long-distance running. Cherry
had written that 'there is something after all rather good
in doing something never done before', but it would be
equally rewarding if Foden could prove that Herodotus'
account was not a myth.

Foden had only been able to get hold of tourist maps
since Turkey's recent invasion of Cyprus had meant that
Ordnance Survey maps of the area were still classified

secrets. With only a skeletal support crew and limited preparation, the group quit when 80 kilometres outside Athens.

For the next two years Foden agitated over their failure and, returning to the maps and the ancient texts, he became convinced that the run could be done with better preparation. He enlisted a support team of ultra-distance runners, then a fledgling sport. He tracked down every 100-kilometre race he could find around Europe, at one stage dragging his wife to the Arctic Circle to compete.

Given clearance from the RAF, Foden was able to acquire a number of small-scale navigation maps. With some military rations, tents, two radios, a camera and a very small financial grant, he set off again in a minibus with a van following. More financial support came through Mike Callaghan, a South African businessman who had seen a notice put up by the British Council in Athens about the attempt. For Foden this was not a race but a challenge – 'to test Herodotus's account'. There would be no prize and no financial reward, simply the knowledge that it could be done. It was a classically eccentric British adventure.

On 8 October the team gathered at the Agora in Athens, the seat of government at the time of the Persian Wars, and headed for the statue of King Leonidas in Sparta, giving them enough time, if needed, to run through a second night and arrive on the Sunday. During three days of reconnaissance, they had plotted a route out of Athens and into the Peloponnese mountains before turning down the Eurotas Valley to Sparta. They spent one day hanging bits of tape from tree branches to mark out the course as best they could. By the time that they were ready to make the attempt, they were almost completely out of money and had to beg for a loan to cover the hotel bill on the final night as they prepared for a dawn start.

The team woke at 4.15 a.m. to find that the hotel cook had not got up as agreed and they had to settle for Mars bars and water instead of a full meal. At 6.30, with a gathering of TV crews, they embarked on their venture as the rising sun silhouetted the Acropolis. They followed their thread of torn sheets and plastic bags, shooing off stray dogs with stones. With the only set of maps in the support van, they periodically got lost as they tried to decipher Greek signposts to places that they had never heard of.

Within an hour the group was starting to come apart. The most experienced ultra-distance runner in the team encouraged the others to slow down, which the TV crews could not understand. By mid-afternoon the temperature had risen from 25 to 35 degrees, and the leading pair were suffering, often having to dive into brambles to avoid oncoming traffic. Unable to reach the drinks station, which was forcibly moved on by the police every time it stopped, they made do with a short swim, having been chased out of a garage car wash by an irate owner. By 11 a.m. their pace had dropped dramatically from 7 to 4 miles an hour. Throughout the afternoon it was virtually impossible to provide the runners with enough to drink and they were unwillingly forced to carry bottles with them. At Corinth, the previous day, they had sighted a café and, as they closed in on it, they began to fantasise about cold drinks, ice cream and doughnuts. Their hearts sank when they found it shut. With that, two of the runners gave up.

By nightfall the team had reached the mountains, where the first kitchen had been set up to feed the runners. Foden lost his compass and, with it, his way, mistaking in the moonlight the sandy bottom of the Inakhosp Valley for the path they had plotted. Like Pan himself emerging to lend courage to Pheidippides that the Athenians would vanquish the Persians, Foden spotted the North Star and knew he was going in the right general direction. Eventually he came across the jeep tracks from their earlier reconnaissance. Once over the worst of the potholes and rocks while being chased by rabid dogs, he picked his way south. By midnight he was at Lyrkia, 96 kilometres from Sparta, where he found the van and more food. By this time Foden was seriously ill, sweating profusely and feeling extremely cold, a common problem for all long-distance runners as their throats swell up from the dry air, and their stomachs cramp painfully, both from the heat and the inability to consume enough calories or glucose. One more runner dropped out and the support crew were becoming increasingly fatigued, the driver having dozed off at one point to wake on the wrong side of the road in the path of an oncoming truck.

As he was able to take in more food, Foden slowly started to recover during his climb of the Bey's Ladder, guided by the reflector tape that had been put up the day before, reaching the summit ahead of schedule. In his euphoria, he tripped and fell on the loose stones and was temporarily reduced to walking again.

By the time the team had reached Tegea they had been on the move for 24 hours, and were desperately dehydrated. Some had started to hallucinate, seeing a black dog in the road that had to be carried to the verge before they could continue.

As Foden closed on Sparta at the top of the drop down into the Eurotas Valley, the first runner having already finished and been taken off to bed, a group of Embassy staff were waiting for him. For the third time he was told that there were only 13 kilometres to go. They asked whether they could run in with Foden, but he was so annoyed at their having been misled that he ran down the mountain as fast as he could to shake them off. On his final climb into Sparta, the statue of King Leonidas emerged and, with it, the reception committee with an olive wreath to crown him. It had taken Foden 37 hours and 58 minutes, and he had lost

6.4 kilograms. All he wanted was a newspaper and a beer to celebrate the fact that he could rightfully claim to have reached Sparta 'the day after' setting off, as had Pheidippides.

Equipped with less support than is now considered standard for a 10-kilometre race, Foden's team had shown that Herodotus' account was at least possible, if never provably accurate. In the hotel room he was too shattered to walk the short distance to the shower and sat down on the bed. The beer was still by the bedside, untouched, when he awoke the next day.

At an impromptu civic reception the following day, Foden was asked to say a few words in response to the team's award of honorary Spartan citizenship. Not knowing how to respond to his Greek hosts, he said that they ought to have a race along the route taken to perpetuate the memory of Pheidippides' run, before declaring that he wanted to run back to Athens as Pheidippides had done, although he was eventually dissuaded from doing so. So was born the Spartathlon.

The idea of running the Spartathlon had harpooned me, and I could not shake it off. I wanted to see whether I could take on something that no one I knew had ever done. I started training again and doubled the programme that I had drawn up to finish my last marathon. But I was newly married. There were other distractions. On Sunday morning I would disappear for hours, hoping that I would exhaust the idea out of myself. I couldn't bring myself even to tell Laurence, my wife, at first. She had encouraged me to run the Paris Marathon – as much, I think, to get me to lose weight before our wedding two months later, since it would make for better photographs – but I feared that she would rebel against this new idea.

I told those who asked that I was running another marathon. I had not even started to comprehend what I was getting into, and I did not want the fuss of having to explain it to others. But by the summer the idea was still agitating me, and I announced that I would be cycling across France to our first wedding of the year. It came as no surprise and there were few questions, but deep within me I hoped that, in the week it would take me to get there, I would starve out the gnawing in my stomach, abandoning the idea of running the Spartathlon as a minor folly.

With a rucksack on my back and maps stuffed down my top, I got into trouble almost the moment I landed in France, having misread the thick red line crossing the river Seine by the port as being open to cyclists. I had to make a 30-mile detour along the banks of the river before I found another bridge, half thinking about swimming the 50 metres of water. No sooner had I crossed the river and was about to restart my journey, already 3 hours behind schedule, than the morning's promise of rain was fulfilled, dissolving the map into a blank canvas.

Five hundred miles later my tyres hissed into Confolens on the boiled tarmac of south-west France. I parked my bicycle against the garden wall and waited for the grand reception that, since lunchtime, I had been imagining would be waiting for me. There was a note from my wife, saying that she had gone to the hairdresser.

Each night I had gorged on steak and beer. Under heavy-lidded eyes, I read about the hunt for Moby Dick across the great waters of the Atlantic and Pacific. I drifted into sleep, dreaming that I too was an explorer heading into waters fraught with danger, imagining that any wrong turn would spell disaster.

The water systems that I knew were the flat river banks of the Thames and the glacial carvings of the Danish fjords, and I had assumed that the easiest way to surmount my challenge was to follow the rivers. For a week I changed gears, stood up on my pedals, sat back down again, got off and walked as I ascended and descended the great crevasses of the French country-side. When, still vacuum-packed within my cycling gear, unshaven and with my hair moulded to the arches of my helmet, I recounted the journey to my father-in-law, assuming that I would astonish him with tales of my adventures, Jean-Louis shook his head in pity. Spreading out the tattered remnants of the map on the kitchen floor, he cast his eye over the hundreds of miles I had passed through and, as though pointing to a corner in his own garden, showed me the route further west that I should have taken to avoid the rivers and, with them, the hills.

It was no use. I could not rid myself of the idea of taking on the Spartathlon. The more exhausted I became, spending 12 hours in the saddle every day, eventually collapsing into a hypoglycaemic sweat as my blood ran out of sugar, the more I wondered: 'Is this what it feels like to run 152 miles?' In the pain that came with every revolution of the pedal, I could not help compare the undoing of my body with what I imagined it would be like to run all day in 37-degree heat and then into the night and over two mountain ranges. Each question was just a prelude to the unanswerable: did I have what it took to run the Spartathlon? To attempt something incredible, just once?

Ten days after I cycled out of Confolens for home, diligently following the route north-west that Jean-Louis had plotted for me, he died from a heart attack in the middle of a field less than a mile from the house in which he had raised his children. He was a vet: healthy, active and watchful of all that he ate and drank. There was nothing to suggest that this would happen. The shutters came down, the car was reversed into the garage and the unwatered plants began to wilt. Around us, babies were being born to friends with whom we could not celebrate. The clocks had stopped and in the space of a few hours a family circle that had been carefully nurtured for thirty years was dissolved and washed away.

The sleepless nights of September were described by an arc of grief that I was impotent to relieve. I had never before witnessed such profound emotional suffering, but as the weeks went by I came to know that those cries in the dark could be rationalised only as a physical exhalation of grief. For as long as the agony was beyond language, it could not be objectified and thereby defused.

It shames me now to think about it, but lying in the dark, trying to coax Laurence to sleep, I started to frame the idea of the Spartathlon in terms of a penance for Jean-Louis's death. I wondered whether, in the Lutheran tradition, the pain I would go through would help draw out the poison of her grief. When I put on my trainers I ran harder and faster than I had ever done before, my lungs burning, my extended stride searing through my whole body. I reasoned that through this pain I would come to better feel how they, she and her family, were suffering, as if through my own pain I would become a more understanding person. That belief was born out of a failure on my part to be able to say what needed to be said, and the fact that there was nothing sensible that could be said.

You might think that I was just looking for an excuse to keep alive the dream of the race. Perhaps this is true. Certainly there ceased to be any coherence in my actions, and more than a little contradiction between my thoughts and actions.

★

'There is only one antidote to mental suffering,' wrote Karl Marx, 'and that is physical pain.' The first person I met who had run the Marathon des Sables told me about it with anguish, having run 151 miles through the 50-degree heat of Morocco to numb the sadness of a rejected marriage proposal. 'As in dying and death, so in serious pain the claims of the body utterly nullify the claims of the world,' wrote Elaine Scarry in *The Body in Pain*.

The motivation that drove Scott, Mallory and Terray to the remotest ends of the earth is in part defined by their pursuit of fear, with which comes an acute sensitivity to death since one false step could end in disaster. For the runner, the hours spent on the road are in part a pursuit of the same connection with our surroundings through pain, which, in its extremity, is equivalent to what is unfeelable in death. Bannister knew, as all runners have known, the scream that comes from the calcification of the bones as we stride out against the wishes of our body. It is this absoluteness, when we learn the extent of our boundaries, that makes running in part a story about experiencing 'the expansive nature of human sentience, the felt-fact of aliveness'. In everyday life, in which we consciously avoid unnecessary hardship, this aliveness is a hypersensitivity that we ordinarily associate with physical gratification. As a result we shy away from painful endeavour in favour of more obvious pleasures.

When runners encounter pain for the first time it is not experienced as a luxuriating hypersensitivity as it is with pleasure that eclipses all else, including the tearing at the hips or the crushing of the legs as they seize up with fatigue. No matter how beautiful the landscape or the number of people cheering you on, nothing can compensate for the terrible burning that creeps through your skin and into your bones when you reach the limits of your capacity. Wherever the pain originates, eventually it occupies every muscle and sinew. And every runner knows the feeling. It displaces all else until 'it seems to become the single broad and omnipresent fact of existence', leaving us spent and exhausted, but in a state of extreme sensitivity in which the body and its surroundings become indistinguishable.

Most of us rarely venture into the mountains, but our palms become sweaty when we contemplate the climber's fear when confronted by the object of his imagination. We can *feel*, in our own limited way, the thrill that defines the experience. As Sir Francis Younghusband wrote of the 1922 assault on Everest, 'we shall eventually get to love the mountain for the very fact that she has forced the utmost out of us, lifted us for one precious moment high above our ordinary life, and shown us the beauty of austerity, power, and purity we should have never known if we had not faced the mountain squarely and battled strongly with her.'

The idea that for runners life is much more intensely

lived on the edge of our own extinction is harder to grasp, since the topography that is being mapped out is purely internal. Cherry came closest to describing the state, but even then, as readers, we are still consumed by the imagined visual or tactile nature of his experience.

But pain takes no object, and like other interior states is impossible to express fully in the external, shareable world. We cannot look out, as Mallory did, and see 'visions of what is mysterious, remote, inaccessible'. As runners, all we can do is map our surroundings, to note, submit and file its geographical extremities. In return we are helped to chart our own physical limitations.

Nietzsche gave the pretence of having got the upper hand by bestowing on it a single name: 'I have given a name to my pain and call it dog. It is just as faithful, just as obtrusive and shameless, just as entertaining, just as clever as any other dog.' Mike Stroud, who ran seven marathons in seven days on seven continents with Sir Ranulph Fiennes, advised his readers to 'make a friend of pain'. There is a warm comfort in this imagined subordination or equality, but we know that it is only temporary.

With good reason we do not ordinarily indulge ourselves with the philosophical virtues that these experiences offer, and perhaps therein lies part of my shame. Instead of going out in search of my own particular kind of suffering, I should have spent that time nursing Laurence's. Everyday life offers enough hardship without our having to seek it voluntarily. With good reason we choose to stay neatly within our comfort zone, walking along the corridors that lead to the lives of our parents.

However, since at least the time of the anarchic Greek hero Alcibiades, we have embraced pain for its own sake and as a means to a greater good. The idea that through it the sufferer becomes a knower, and it is through that knowledge that we feel most alive was repeated by every ultra-distance runner I have ever met. I have heard some of them say that, as a result of the years of training that they have undergone, they have felt as though they were becoming superhuman, 'able to run through walls'. This may be true, but in fact the pain of running those thousands of miles leads to a hypersensitivity to their bodies, in which every flex and nuance of their steps is registered as a continual agitation in the brain. Through the exhilaration we become better acquainted with the limits of our moral and physical capacities.

Although pain may seem to take over the whole world while we are in the midst of it, for those around us it seems distinctly unreal. There are no physical scars, there is no totem of suffering. It all occurs deep beneath the skin, is not available to sensory confirmation and is worse for that. We can know what it is like only when we feel it for ourselves. And the beauty of running is that this revelation of empathy through pain is something that all of us can achieve, whether we are accomplished athletes or not. To listen to the ultra-distance runners returning from their extraordinary journeys requires an acknowledgement that there is a radical subjectivity to their suffering, which language alone cannot communicate.

Whatever pain achieves, it does so in part through its outward unshareability. English, wrote Virginia Woolf, 'can express the thoughts of Hamlet and the tragedy of Lear . . . but let a sufferer try to describe a pain . . . and language at once runs dry'. The agony of the runner, as his legs turn to ebony and his muscles are calcified by cruel hills, is the agony of grief that words can no longer express.

If you have run great distances you will know this feeling well. You will have waited in vain for the pain to pass, for vitality to be restored to your body, and you will have grimaced in horror at its absoluteness. But deep down you love it because it is, in part, for this very experience that you have trained so hard. If you have seen such a face from the barricades, and have not suffered as these runners have suffered, salute them. What they are experiencing in that silent scream is epic, beyond comprehension, and deserves to be considered in silent reverence as they pass you by.

3

Migration

Maybe it is because I was born by its banks, but nearly all my life I have been drawn to the waters of the Thames. And it was here that I covered most of the 6,000 miles I ran in training for the Spartathlon, enough to complete its length over thirty times.

Through the winter months I arrived at the office while it was still dark and put in an hour from Hammersmith to Kew Bridge and back before work. In the spring I would leave early and cover 20 miles upstream before the weekend had begun. I ran, showered, changed and dressed in a routine that I followed twice, sometimes three times a day, covering 18 miles daily, sometimes more. In between those runs I tried to retain some semblance of a working routine as I went between meetings with wet hair, sometimes barefoot, itching for 5.30 to come around so I could go out and do it all over again.

For those who live beside the Thames there is an inward and intimate association. The river teaches patience, endurance and vigilance. For some of us, it is an unavoidable physical and psychological presence, a metaphor for our lives as transitory individuals. It is 'within us – liquid history', wrote John Burns, as it contains the world around us. For Thoreau, by looking into any water 'the beholder measures the depths of his own nature'. In the river's state of perpetual becoming, it allows each new visitor to return to its banks and find their own stories, as if in a looking glass. In the same way that the Thames incorporates the story of a nation, it was here that I started to unravel my own myth – to separate fact from fiction – and to make sense of my own place in the scheme of things.

I was born in Westminster Hospital, now a government building, on Horseferry Road, which leads to one of the first bridges to have been constructed over the great psychological divide between north and south London. On one side there was sophistication, order and governance. On the other, industry and bedlam. Although millions of Londoners traverse the river every day, it is a passage of water that is difficult to reach, touch or smell. So omnipresent has it always been that we rarely pay attention to it, unless it brings forth novel stories like that of the bottlenose whale in 2006, or clouds of smoke and steam when a tanker drives into one of the bridges. Commuters move across it swiftly, their eyes fixed ahead, and try to avoid getting too close to the liquid mass. They will laugh at tourists who venture gamely upon it, because for many Londoners the river leads nowhere and they have no use for it. However, if we stopped for only a moment to consider, we would realise that it has a story to tell about our own creation.

It was in *The Principles of Psychology* that William James first evoked the idea of a 'stream of consciousness' in which 'every definite image of the mind is steeped . . . in the free water that flows around it'. The river's power is as difficult to articulate fully as with the swelling tide its hypnotic rhythm is hard to decode. Yet, for this reason, it has meant so much to so many different people over the centuries. For some it has been a psychological prop. Shelley felt that the river entered his head, and saw it as an image of human consciousness that represented the flow of being. Byron was enamoured enough of it to submerge himself in it, and from Lambeth Bridge he would swim for miles, feeling its tempo replicating the ebb and flow of his own imagination.

Just as our personalities change and mature with time, so too is the Thames not a single river, since its personality alters in the course of its journey. The adolescent rapids of the upper stream above Lechlade slowly give way to a more melodic and ponderous consideration as the river passes through its middle life at Oxford, then flows through London and out to the sea.

What starts with purity under a tree at its source in the Cotswolds ends in a dark, foul stew defiled by greed and excess in the broad reaches of the commercial world.

'In this regress it is the paradigm of human life and human history,' wrote Peter Ackroyd, the historian of all things populated. Sir Walter Raleigh considered the river a model of human destiny: 'The freight of time grew ever more complex and wearisome as it proceeded from its source; human life had become darker and deeper, less pure and more susceptible to the tides of affairs.' The temptation to see the river as a metaphor for our own journey, for escape – both temporary and permanent, for consciousness and for human history – becomes delightfully overwhelming.

Some might reply that the river only reflects, that it holds no form of its own, that it contains no intrinsic meaning, and that our belief that it has a discrete personality stems from our tendency to anthropomorphise. But even if we are, like Narcissus, peering into its realms, seeing only ourselves and the story of our own becoming, what a story it is!

Running too is laden with metaphor. And yet, in itself, it is so simple an action – after all, it is just a repetition of the formula of putting one foot in front of the other – that few remember actually being taught how to run. All that most people can recall was that there came a moment years ago when they put out a foot to stop themselves falling over and kept going. Watch how children run across an open field, clumsy at first – each leg reaching out to counter the force of gravity that pulls them irresistibly to the ground – but with time the limbs move freely in innocent delight, unclouded by conscious thought. And yet we know that it is more complicated than this.

'Running! If there's any activity happier, more exhilarating, more nourishing to the imagination, I can't think what it might be,' wrote Joyce Carol Oates. 'In running the mind flies with the body; the mysterious effervescence of language seems to pulse in the brain, in rhythm with our feet and the swinging of our arms.' As we grow into adults we start to think too much about the action, overloading it with purpose and meaning that it does not intrinsically have. If only we were able to switch off our rational thought processes when we run, then it would remain as uncomplicated an experience as it is in childhood.

As the brain is also a muscle, when we run the blood pumping around our system fills it with additional oxygen. The mind is fuelled but at no extra cost, since all we have to concentrate on is keeping one foot going down after the other. With the oxygen, our imagination comes alive, shaking loose all the baggage that we thought we had left behind at home. What can come if we are lucky, when we spend time on our feet, is a clarity of thought, as we work through the issues that have set us down on the road in the first place. If I could go some way to recapturing that moment in which the mind is disconnected from the body, regaining some of that innocence of childhood and just run unblinkered, then I might stand a chance of surviving the Spartathlon.

To be able to run for 36 hours, without stopping, as I would have to in Greece, I knew that I had to maintain this state of transfixion. I needed to learn how to wash out all metaphor, all meaning and all imagination, and just run. As I contemplated entering the race, I was thinking about it too much, and the more I thought about it the more inconceivable a proposition it became. While I was running to train my body, I also had to train myself mentally to withstand the inevitable moments of despondency. 'Ninety per cent of the training for the race is in your head,' said John Foden when we had sat down over lunch to talk about his experience of the Spartathlon. 'The legs are much easier to train – just put in the miles. The mind is more complicated.' It either had to be subjugated to the will, or cast adrift from the body.

Without imagination there would be no metaphor. Most days when running along the Thames, I was able to keep my eyes fixed firmly on the next bend in the river as I stuck to my task, my mind emptied of the day's turbulence. On those days I would return home truly exhilarated, light. There is no better word for it – free. On those days I could ask myself what had been going through my mind and I would say, with all honesty, that it had been void of all thought. I had run with nothing more than my feet. I was pure motion.

While the records I made of the miles I had run were a note of the physical exertion that I was putting myself through, on their own they recorded nothing of the mental states in which I left and returned to the house. After Jean-Louis's funeral Laurence and I retreated into our grief and barely saw anyone except when it was unavoidable. September became October, then November and we adopted a kind of self-imposed hibernation. Friends telephoned to check on us, but we left the phone unanswered, and soon they stopped calling altogether.

When we did leave the house, it was to fly to France to be with Laurence's mother, Marie-Jo, as we tried to work out what should happen next. We spent ten days in France with her over Christmas and they were some of the coldest and clearest days I have ever known. I made myself scarce when it was needed, and as much as I could I maintained the daily routine of running 18 miles along the country paths close to the family house. Sometimes I could feel that I was just running, my step light as it bounced over the loose stones and frozen mud. At other times, the weight of their grief was too much and I would have to slow to a walk as I collected myself before starting up again, running harder and faster than I had ever done before in an attempt to dispel the fog in my head.

It took months for me to realise how overwhelmingly difficult it was to summon the state of pure motion that I was in search of. I only had to catch the last of the sun striking through the green flesh of the leaves and a choking would take me by the throat. No matter how far I was into the run, I would suddenly have to resist the urge to stop, finding all at once that I could not understand the meaning of anything. I could explain nothing I heard or saw, nor what I was doing out here, even though the demand for an explanation had, until then, been met. I knew that sometimes – perhaps after a bad day in the office – I was guilty of taking the metaphor too far by projecting my own instabilities onto the world, in a bizarre psychological version of the pathetic fallacy of the Romantics which saw human emotions reflected in every minute working of nature. And if I was feeling sentimental or just plain exhausted, as I ran in the dark, alone, worrying the badgers making their setts, sometimes I was conscious of an ancient, oppressive melancholy, brooding over the river. But I challenge anyone not to feel a test of nerve – of wanting to be elsewhere, or at least thought of – when you are out running on a Friday night when friends and lovers are gathered somewhere else after a long week at work.

Those miles represented running as a metaphor lived out. Even though I had lived almost my entire life close to this river, I had never seen it through these eyes before. What overwhelmed me in those moments of symbolism, as I made the mistake of starting to think too much, was really my struggle to keep all my history in my head at once. Directly upstream was the house I had journeyed from and the place that my parents still call home. From there a long, unbroken chain seemed to stretch to the bend of the river on which I stood, studying the light refracting through the leaves.

Every family has its secrets, and if you too decide to run just to see how far you can go, then you will inevitably have to come to terms with the history that brought you there. When you spend so much time contemplating your lot, it is imperative that you learn to defend yourself against the equally inevitable mental corrosion that will follow. This includes believing that these extraordinary challenges – of which the Spartathlon was but one, albeit the toughest – are nothing more than futile gestures.

For runners the task is simple. We just need to rid ourselves of all the symbolism and metaphor in order to become pure kinetic energy. We must unharness ourselves from the rubble that we drag around with us, free ourselves from imagination, and learn, as we did as children, what it is to run with our feet alone. To know how to do this requires an understanding of that past. You will know where your story begins. This is mine.

We moved to Oxford in 1984 when my younger brother and I, aged six, were lifted out of a world of cracked pavements, double-decker buses and windows cross-hatched with iron bars, into a world of quilted fields in a sea of green pigment that became visible all at once as you crossed the county border along the M40. It was on those final car journeys out of London, when my parents were deciding where we would live, that we peered out of the window to see red kites scatter high above us, wildlife that was unimaginable in the city, their rusty tails luminous against the attack of white under their wings. We watched them hover, holding our breath, before they dived at their prey.

For John Wycliffe, Oxford was 'the house of God and the gate of heaven'. Many of its residents still see it as a kingdom in microcosm, incorporating the ancient and the new, the pastoral and the commercial. As a site of power and prosperity it was once considered an island fortress, making it unwilling to move away from its past.

Oxford is almost entirely surrounded by water. To the east the river Cherwell runs into the Thames to mix with the meandering Isis to the west, whose vapours hang all year long over the flat fields of Port Meadow until winter freezes them into a sickly fog. As a teenager, Joseph Turner came here to sketch some of his first landscapes. Though he returned repeatedly to clarify his own metaphor for the nation in flux, those first sketches from the hills south of the city are so lightly drawn that they give the impression that he had been scared off by the dank air.

Of the city and those same vapours, Max Beerbohm wrote, 'that lotus-land saps the will power, the power of action. But in doing so, it clarifies the mind, makes larger the vision, gives, above all, that playful and caressing suavity of manner which comes from a conviction that nothing matters except ideas . . . There is nothing in England to be matched with what lurks beneath the vapours of these meadows, that mysterious, invisible spirit.' By moving to Oxford we were entering a mythical dominion, shrouded in the 'mild miasmal air' of Beerbohm's painfully sentimental love story.

The Thames at Oxford has a new personality, juxtaposed between two worlds. Upstream, towards its source, it is called the Isis, and is a place of innocence and purity. Downstream, it moves towards the noise and corruption of the capital. From the fault line that runs through Oxford London does not quite rush up, as Peter Ackroyd would have us believe, but it is always around the next corner. When one contrasts the calm and contemplative lapping of the river upstream with what it becomes when it reaches the sea, it seems impossible that it is the same river. At Oxford, it can be shallow and clear, green rather than brown. A hand beneath the surface would not disappear as it would if we were able to get close enough to touch it at Battersea. Nor were these peaceful upper reaches sought out by Dickens' suicides, although Zuleika Dobson's melodramatic lovers walked these banks as they considered what life would be like without her. For all who have contemplated the river here, it seems to flow steadily towards a brighter, better future, untainted by its noxious consistency further downstream. Here it is beloved of poets, who worshipped it, preferring its sweetness to the bubonic Thames of London. For William Morris, the Thames at Oxford was simply Utopia.

At the bottom of the garden of the house that we moved into was the suggestion of a stream, pompously named Cromwell's Ditch. It lapped so tepidly for most of the year that it seemed to cling to its bed, unlike the wide, gallant reach that it eventually flowed into south of Oxford. But to two young boys the soft air held the promise of a wilder childhood than the pollution of the great capital, and we immediately set about constructing a world of pirates and galleons on the static water.

We had been brought here in part to get away from the noise of the big city. Within a year of our leaving London, a girl had been raped and a policeman murdered less than 100 metres from our former house, something that repeatedly shocked my parents in the retelling. For my father, though, the move was also a homecoming. He was born in the middle of the war while his father had been stationed at RAF Benson, before being drafted to Norfolk, from which the Wellington bombers lumbered over the Channel to Dresden. My father was nine months old when his father was killed, and his mother moved from their caravan on the airbase to be closer to his family. She was nineteen when he died and pregnant with their first daughter. Five years later she returned to Oxford. She married her lodger and the family moved first to Nottingham, then, in 1958, to a house in Bristol where she would die forty years later.

She had always assumed that, in retirement, they would come back to Oxford. But whether they just never got around to it, or had become so entrenched in the corners of their relationship to consider the idea, it is not entirely clear why they never did. What is certain is that she never stopped loving her first husband. That became less obvious to see, as much of the fight had gone out of her and her second husband by the time they were grand-parents, but after each meal they would retreat to different parts of the house, intent on having as little to do with each other as possible. My father left it for me to decide whether her nagging desire to return to Oxford and the refusal to let it happen, were both driven by the same ghost that haunted their marital bed, or whether he himself was too painful a reminder of the past.

That my father had been born, quite literally, up the road from the house we moved to came as no surprise. I did not doubt him when he said that we had moved there because he and my mother had wanted to give my brother and me the freedom of the open fields. He had never been one for big cities. His office window at home looked out on the river – and at weekends we would find him there, paper scattered over the desk, gazing at the water. What became more true, though, especially after his mother died, was that he had come back to be closer to his father. It was as if he had been looking for a childhood that he only vaguely remembered and in the process he was starting again, giving us the infancy that he had never had.

For twenty-four years, until my parents moved again, Oxford was *terra cognita*, and there was a totemic nature to the landscape of my youth. The river offered a deep sense of settlement and belonging, conscious of the passing of its seasons as we grew up. In winter it would flood and freeze, the dusty ice revealing the stalking of a fox, or the patter of confused birds that had skidded across the surface as they came in to land. In the summer boys would come in boats and hunt for pike, hauling them out before clubbing them to death with a paddle, fishy water flailing up from the rubbery flesh. When my parents moved out of the house, I had by then long since left it and all those memories became obscured, penned in behind someone else's fence and relegated to the kind of abstraction that meant that neither the river nor my childhood was mine any longer. It was as if those years had never happened.

At Christmas and again at Easter I returned to visit my parents and in the early mornings took to running along the flooded bank where the river passed through Oxford, breathing deeply the refreshing lightness of my early memories. It had been so long since I had last thought of them that it was like being in a foreign country that I had read about but never visited. Not only did the memories themselves surprise me, but I also viewed them, as though for the first time, with great clarity, seeing more sharply the story I had come in search of. When I returned home, steam rising from me in the winter frost, the sight of my parents made me think, mistakenly, that I understood everything that there was to know about them.

My river rises in a field known as Trewsbury Mead, and is impossible to get to by water. The Thames' pre-eminent historian Fred Thacker wrote that 'all you get in arid seasons is the infrequent pool of still and not always sweet water. One's first emotions are almost to tears.' In the summer the exact spot can be difficult to find. It had been disappointing fair-weather visitors for years.

With Thacker's words in mind I looked for it in midwinter, the sky white with frost, after a week of rain that had made the Thames burst its banks further down-stream. I walked across soft fields, reading the cryptic lines from my guide book as though it was some ancient text: 'half a mile from the main road cross the railway track and follow the dip in the field to a giant Ash'. Wind-blasted and stricken, its branches crane over the bubbling pool, clear and magical. A post marked the 184 miles to the Thames Barrier, but there was no sign of the cement rendition of Old Father Thames made by Rafaelle Monti in 1854 to mark the river's source. There used to be a wall here too, but now there was only a collection of rough stones. To be standing on this spot was to experience a peculiar vertigo. No matter how imperceptible it is, from this point, visitors are always figuratively peering towards the great city and the river's mouth at Gravesend.

I circled the spot as though its story would come to me all at once if I looked hard enough and spent the morning following the water out of the field until it found its momentum, transforming into a gurgling rush. Barely a mile away it had already begun a downward trajectory as it gathered pace, carving through the fields towards the sea.

The banks were bloated with rain, but I changed into my running kit because I wanted to see if it would feel any different to run here rather than further downstream. My feet got soaked immediately in the cold, wet grass but it was pleasant to be moving so slowly through the boggy terrain while the stream sped past me with childish exuberance.

Hilaire Belloc, whose house faced the water at Battersea Bridge, noticed that above Oxford there is evident reluctance amongst those who live by it to move with the economic changes 'wrought by the foundations lower down the stream'. It is as though civilisation cannot pass through the fifty locks around Oxford, keeping the pastoral idyll pure of the contamination downstream. There are even very few houses up here, which means no funnelling of the river, and to run along these banks is to step back hundreds of years.

Until the Great War, four-fifths of the population of the Upper Thames lived and died within 10 miles of their birthplace. Its people were not migratory, nor were they curious in the slightest about where the river led. This much, at least, they have in common with the commuters downstream. For them it was just a small body of water that disappeared around the furthest corner. There was no psychological or metaphorical pollution, and they had no use for it beyond its function for their survival.

In its kinetic energy, the river is a living symbol of Miłosz's philosophy of freedom 'which consists in being aware that a choice made now, today, projects itself backwards and changes our past actions'. The way in which it flowed up here near the source, free and untainted, was how I would need to learn to run to survive the Spartathlon.

All human life is muddled by error, and my family's story is no different. To begin with, as I peered down the years like a voyeur through dense bramble, it was difficult to make out why my mother's family had moved from Germany to Denmark before she left for England in 1969. It was not simply that my mother concealed her reasons for leaving. To begin with, I was trying to apply a tidy logic to the family's movements, seeing coherence where there was contradiction, and not realising that stories were out of sequence, involving elements that were not only displaced but seemed to have acquired a significance they hadn't really earned. My family history was written in pure pidgin – full of slang, neologisms, mimicry and deception.

Even when both her parents were dead, my mother only ever alluded obliquely to her past, our past, resistant to explaining why she had left Denmark so suddenly. The only way to navigate that past was to plunge into it myself. We all have our secrets, the hidden stories from long ago that rush us downstream, and for the most part we do well to leave them alone. As spring entered my lungs and I had started to log over 100 miles a week in training, I flew out to Denmark, alone, in the hope of finding some definition to my mother's history.

Many families have a relative who has traced their ancestors in hope of finding hidden gold. As my parents cleared out boxes accumulated over two and a half decades to move house, we found the sun-bleached document, which could fit neatly into a back pocket, that revealed the route that my mother's family had taken from the industrial town of Haagen in Germany to Vejle in Denmark. There were photographs, too, shielded from a century of light, of austere and incorruptible *herren* and *frauen*, with strong Teutonic names like Fritz, Carl, Bertha and Gottfried. Their fixed expressions, sitting in a favourite armchair, or standing with hands thrust into tailored suit pockets, suggested ideals of workmanship and moral rectitude. But who they were remained a complete mystery.

We were the offspring of migrants, the family tree was clear on that. An argument over rights to water needed to power an iron foundry in Haagen, south-west of Hamburg, had forced my great-great-grandfather Fritz Brinker to look north, where the water was, for work. In 1842 he arrived in Haraldskjaer, Vejle, to take a job as the manager of an iron factory. Six months later, he sent for his wife, Juliane, and his year-old son, Carl. It took her four weeks, walking beside the horse-drawn cart that contained everything they owned, to reach him.

The Brinkers prospered. Following the French uprising in 1848, German forces invaded Denmark returning again in 1864 to lay claim to it. Halle Hess, a distant relative, who had melted lead into soldiers for my brother and me, claimed that there was a true story that a cousin from Haagen had saluted Fritz and Juliane from horseback as he rode through the town with the army. But by then they, like many other migratory Germans, had become nationalised Danes.

I had a whole day to peel through before I was due to meet my cousin Henrik in Flensborg on the German border, where he worked as the Danish Consul General. The solid building that he called home looked down from a cliff face over the town and into the shipping channels that had once brought so much wealth to the region. The house had been built as an emblem of that wealth, but now its four-foot walls were used to keep out the political drama of tyres burnt in protest against the controversial Danish cartoons, a reminder that boundaries still existed between two countries that were essentially united.

With my eyes streaming with fatigue from the too-early start that morning, I drove first to our former summer cottage in Henne on the west coast. I had had no intention of doing so when I had got on the plane, but the moment I got into the hire car the compulsion overcame me. As it was a weekday, the roads were empty and I rolled down the main street to the beach just as the bakery and supermarket were readied for the day. The sand was wet and cold, and the wind cut across the damp banks of dunes. I stepped down behind them to the spot where my brother and I had spied on the weekend's new arrivals, then drove to the cottage. From the roof the flag kicked in the wind. Someone was home. I parked further up the road and watched. I had no business being here, and I felt a slight queasiness at being in an unfamiliar scene in a place I knew so well. I wanted to be submerged in the rich nostalgia of my childhood, but all I could summon was the loneliness of self-imposed exile. So I reclined the seat, pulled my hat down over my eyes and fell asleep.

There is something very special about this country. I drove across the flat, wide countryside, first to the east coast, before turning sharply south to pick up the motorway that cleaved through the country towards Flensborg and then Hamburg. The landscape around me seemed to be constantly trembling; the grass in the fields or the water on the fjords – everything signalled the wind's presence. The light in the spring was soft and mutable, the sky itself alive, constantly in flux. It would have been through these fields of corn and wheat that Juliane would have trod with her cart a century and a half before, turning her back on the only life she knew, understanding that she would probably never set foot in Germany again.

When I arrived, the length of Henrik's official dining table was already covered with photographs, birth certificates and graphs illustrating the peaks and troughs of our family fortunes. Along with a portrait of Juliane, there was my great-grandfather Gottfried's business card too: his name, official title and *Vejle*, written in the bottom right-hand corner. Gottfried had imported timber from the forests of Finland when the demand was high and then, as the town grew, coal to power the ovens and the steamers. It is his name that is faded to grey on the steel frames of the old cranes that sit idle in Vejle's port. There was money, and souvenirs too from a journey in the 1920s to the battlefields at Dieppe. The small-town businessman had wanted to see the world. In one photograph, the round-faced Gottfried is dressed like a man who never went anywhere without his valet, whose bicep he is gripping with the huge slab of his hand.

'There are some things that I will leave for your mother to tell you about,' Henrik said, as we put away the papers before dinner. He did not blink as he assessed how much information I already had. He was reluctant to explain much further. As little as I knew about the family's improved social standing, I knew far less about the emotional instability of their relationships. There was only one clue I had to go on – my mother's confession that she had never wanted to return to Denmark to live.

'Gottfried and Erik, your grandfather, had a complicated relationship. Gottfried sat on your grandfather, and that was one of the problems. He never had a chance to, you know, develop as a person.' He wouldn't say more.

We put on our coats against the coastal breeze and went to dinner. When we returned he showed me the scorch marks from the siege laid by the furious locals over the cartoons of Allah, then wished me goodnight. I went to my room in the north-facing tower that looked out over the Danish border, the Baltic and a harbour full of the kind of fleets that a hundred years ago would have brought Gottfried his timber.

I had deliberately saved the trip to Vejle until last, hoping to savour the anticipation for as long as possible, since it had been seven years since I had last been there on the occasion of my grandmother's funeral. I passed her old flat and the house where my mother had been born. The traffic rolled through the town centre over the inter-connecting railway lines that curved through the street to the docks and had once been part of a network reaching out across Denmark. The port, from which Gottfried's ships had set sail to bring coal from Newcastle, had been empty of the hundred-tonne tankers for a generation. Now it was owned by developers and work on a new block of flats, with an astonishing view out towards the Baltic, was starting on the waterfront. The very real presence of Gottfried dominated my sense of place: it was like slipping into a pocket of the past. I didn't know who I was here, but I didn't need to know. I had returned to a place and time where I had not yet been born.

In the hotel room, reproduction pictures hung on the wall from the level of the electric sockets near the floor to within an inch of the frieze. Kitsch landscapes of idyllic pastoral scenes had been placed with great care next to modernist still-life paintings and blurred Parisian café settings, as though the connection was entirely apparent. The bed was too long for the room and the mattress gave way beneath my weight like melting butter, so that I clambered out of it the next morning as though from a bath.

There are no short cuts to becoming an ultra-distance runner and the single most important lesson I had learnt after six months of training was to log as many miles a week as possible. Eighty was a minimum, 100 preferable. I had not run the previous day and, even with only 24 hours' rest, the dull warmth of extended fatigue had lifted and my step felt light, my movement fluid once again. But it was not just a question of the miles. In preparation for each marathon I had run, I had only ever increased the weekly mileage, letting the exercise take care of my excess weight. Although I am not built like a long-distance runner, I did have control over my calorie intake, and if I was going to have any reasonable chance of success in the Spartathlon, I needed to be as light as possible.

Lunch every day was now a bowl of lentils cooked with carrots and celery that I would eat in small mouthfuls while getting dressed after the midday run. In the evening I would have a slab of steak and little else. The effects were dramatic and immediate with 2, 3, 4 then 5 kilos falling off in the first few months. The result, though, was inevitable and I was continually famished on top of being physically exhausted by the change of regime.

Each time I felt myself waver, something that happened more frequently when I was away from home, I would have to sit down with a bowl of fruit and remind myself that everything in my life was now pointing towards a single goal. Just as I had returned to my past to see how it had got me to where I now was, my every act was contributing to a single narrative that would conclude with the Spartathlon. This was my life now, and it was in those moments that I realised I was becoming a runner.

I had left Flensborg later than expected and was already late for lunch with Inge and Halle Hess, but I had prepared my excuses. Without unpacking my bags, I changed into my running kit and tilted out along the fjord.

Inge and Halle lived 4 miles out of Vejle at the bottom of the road named after Halle's grandfather Christian. The living-room window was a single pane of glass the size of a small swimming pool that looked out over the fjord where boats would race in the summer. Inge had once swum the kilometre width, her husband up ahead in a rowing boat looking out for danger beneath the water's surface.

As Gottfried Becker-Christensen bought the timber and coal to fuel the town, so Christian Hess, another descendant of Juliane's, had made the stoves. But Christian had been the wiser of the two and had made provision when trade started to shift away from their nineteenth-century business. The herringbone-style floor was evidence enough of that, as he had bought it from Gottfried when my mother's family had been forced to sell Gottfried's town house after his death, the last remnant of Christian and Gottfried's legacy as two of the most important people in Vejle.

While we talked, Halle opened three boxes with

Becker-Christensen stamped across them like a police file, and Inge brought in a huge home-baked cake covered in icing. This was the kind of dilemma I had hoped to avoid by bringing with me a packed lunch of lentils to eat in the hotel, because while I craved the sugar, I had to stick to my diet. I did not want to be rude, or have to explain the connection between uncovering my family history and running the Spartathlon, so I took as small a slice as possible and ate it slowly, while Halle cut himself second and third helpings.

Many of the family papers were duplicates of those shown to me by Henrik but they included a photo album that I had not seen before. When I peeled back the silk paper on the brown pages, which had clearly not been turned since the album had been completed, there was a photograph of my mother with her family on the day of her confirmation. I could not understand why it was here. I had never seen it before, but it felt as though I should have done, since the photograph on the opposite page was one of me sitting in her lap on the balcony of my grandmother's apartment. Although I had not looked at it for years, I knew this photograph well. It also belonged in a slim family album that lived in our drawing room and was brought out at idle moments on Christmas Day when no one knew what else to do.

Aged fourteen, my mother sits on brown satin furniture in the family house. Through the window and out of shot, the exploding colours of the sixties revolution are about to light up the sky. Inside, the dark veneer of the heavy oak and lace-covered tables bore witness to the last vestiges of a nineteenth-century moral code that the family had been built on and could not let go of. It was a scene straight out of the pages of Thomas Mann's family epic, *Buddenbrooks*.

With Gottfried widowed and only a year from death, 'things' – as my mother referred to the past to obscure it better – had started to unravel. But my mother's smile in the photograph revealed nothing of that. For the moment she was protected. I experienced a real pain: the sort that stabs at you when something beautifully and intricately made is threatened.

Gottfried had married into the new merchant class when he took Bertha as his wife in 1903, at the age of twenty-nine. He gave his name to the business a year later and, by 1914, he had bought two steamers, *Hamlet* and *Crown Prince*, with Christian Hess. Even the crash of the Reichsmark in 1925 did not alter his fortunes or the scale of his ambition. As a mark of his own import-ance he commissioned a titan's house for the summer months, to be built overlooking the fjord by an archi-tect from Copenhagen, with a tower belatedly added at Gottfried's request.

The business continued until his death in 1962 after which it went bankrupt, was put into administration and was sold off, with the last family signature appearing on

1 January 1970. The rise and decline of the Budden-brook family, which, unlike my own family's, took place over several generations, is encapsulated in a single sentence from a scene at the dinner table: 'A general pause in the conversation ensued, lasting for half a minute, while the company looked down at their plates and pondered the fortunes of the brilliant family who had built and lived in the house and then, broken and impoverished, had left it.'

Much of my reason for delving into my family's past was to put its ups and downs into perspective. By doing so I hoped to find out who Gottfried was and thereby understand the legacy he wanted to leave behind and how I fitted in. This was difficult to grasp until I realised that Gottfried would have known the story of Juliane walking alongside the cart all the way from Germany, and yet the year before he died he would have heard Kennedy announce that NASA was going to send men to the moon. I still struggle to see how anyone could hope to reasonably understand a world that moved so fast, or even that it was the same world.

Gottfried's funeral was statesman-like in grandeur, a celebration of the passing of not just a man, but the prosperity of a small town. Hundreds of people lined the streets as the carriage was drawn to the quiet grave-yard where Bertha, having frequently been taken off to a sanitorium to calm her nerves, had been laid to rest ten years earlier. In Vejle the story of the family's decline played itself out in a single generation, leaving later ones to put the family back together again. By the time Gottfried died, the damage had been done.

As the skies darkened Halle drove me back to the hotel and asked again whether I was sure that I did not want to stay for dinner. I refused politely, explaining that I was seeing other family friends, but as soon as I got into the hotel room I undressed and got back into my running kit that was still soaking wet from earlier that day.

Just as it was only now that I was showing real interest in the narrative that had brought me metaphorically downstream, it was only because I was running real distances that I became interested in my body as a physical object. While the lentils and the miles were sculpting my muscles into stone, the definitions around my stomach and chest becoming sharper, it was when I checked in to the physiotherapist every couple of months to loosen up my joints that I started to really understand what was going on under my skin.

For an hour and a half the physiotherapist would pummel up and down each leg and through my lower back, milking out the residue of the tension that was both a leftover of the pain that left me prostrate as a teenager, as well as the result of not stretching sufficiently, or sometimes at all, after each run. As she took each muscle between her fingers, she explained its fibrous connection to the rest of me, clarifying for me what was going on as my body was transformed. Each time I stepped down from the massage table, I understood better the engineering that made runners out of sinew and tissue.

While she kneaded my muscles like dough she talked of the runners she had had under her thumbs, and described in detail the damage, tension and pain she could feel through their skin. The people she treated were much more natural runners than I could hope to be, and she described working their bodies with great delight saying that the best of them were more like gymnasts than runners, equipped with internal gyroscopes that made them ideally suited to covering long distances over rough terrain. Her most regular client was a teacher who ran the 145-mile Grand Union Canal race from Birmingham to London every year. It took him nearly twelve months to recover. Every month he would come to see her, hoping that she would be able to help heal the scars he had inflicted on the tissue deep within his body.

The stories she told were a reminder that as phenomenal as these ultra-distance athletes are, they are made of flesh and bone. Theirs were bodies that still corroded under pressure. She knew that I wanted to be one of them, and she did not dissuade me, only warned of the consequences. She had never met anyone who had run the Spartathlon, and she could not hide how curious she was to see what it would do to me, and she pressed me to come and see her after I returned.

Putting on my head torch and fluorescent jacket, I ran back out along the fjord, into the forests above the house where my mother had been brought up, before returning to a bowl of cold lentils, a banana and a cereal bar that had been squashed at the bottom of my bag.

I only ever heard my grandfather Erik speak to call out my grandmother's name, 'Sonja!' which came out like a solitary clap at a school play, startling the room. Bedstefar, as we called him – grandfather in Danish – would sit at the end of the table while we ate, thunking his false teeth against his gums as he poured himself a soda water. While Bedstemor cut up his dinner, he would stare at us, unblinkingly, a neat row of pills ready in front of him, counted off like beads on an abacus. I had heard it said that alcohol had damaged his brain, but as he sat at the end of the table his mind did not seem lost, just elsewhere, as he observed us with watery eyes. Perhaps he was still thinking of his father, Gottfried, of a death never fully accepted – a forgiveness for the pain caused, never properly given.

One of three brothers, Erik had been brought into the family business in his thirties. By then, one of Gottfried's steamships had sunk in the Second World War and the shifting markets that Gottfried was not quick enough to follow were returning Vejle to its former ordinariness. The few sheets of paper that denoted the father finally passing on the baton to the sons were not handed over until 1958, the fourth year that Gottfried had resorted to sending silk underwear to the bank manager's wife to hold off the bank's calling in the loans.

Bedstefar inherited the title of Consul, awarded to Gottfried for looking after Finnish and Greek seamen who docked in Vejle during the war. Along with the great family Bible, Gottfried had given Bedstefar a gold chain, which he wore around his neck, at the end of which hung a small medallion with a dismal design on an irregularly hatched surface. It may or may not have been meant as a reminder of where the family had started, but it certainly denoted who was responsible for its fortunes. Bedstefar had little use for it, nor for the place where his family had come from: a flat, humid marshland in northern Germany. I never saw the chain again after he died, although under his pillow we did find a key to a wardrobe filled with silk shirts and hand-crafted watches that no one had ever known existed.

Even once the world had passed them by, Bedstefar's invitation to join the business had come with the under-standing that his was to be a passive contribution. He struggled to cope with a father who would neither let go nor die, not that he knew what he would do when that happened. The titan's summerhouse had gone; the town house would go too, soon enough, filling Erik with an impotent rage. His greatest rebellion would have been to deny his father by refusing to have children. Since the old man had shored up his relationship with the banks to keep him solvent until he died, Gottfried's only concern was for his legacy. To have gone childless would have been to take responsibility since it would have denied the old man his legacy. With no children, there would have been no need to keep moving, no urge to wield the kitchen knife in rage.

Instead Erik and Sonia had three children, who escaped under Sonia's guidance to the Arctic Circle, Canada and, much later and last of all, England. There was Erik's alcoholism, Bach – listened to alone with the door closed – and talk of a divorce that Bedstemor knew Gottfried would never allow.

My mother was sent away at the age of sixteen, first to boarding school, then to Paris, before taking the boat to England where she arrived with a suitcase in one hand and a letter of introduction in the other. 'All through childhood we grow towards life, and then in adolescence, at the height of life, we begin to grow towards death,' wrote Rebecca Solnit in *A Field Guide to Getting Lost*. Just at that moment when my mother should have been embracing life, a comfortable routine and putting down her own roots, she was sent into exile.

Halle took me into the basement, the stairs creaking in symphony with his legs, and unlocked the door. The electric light revealed the dusty accumulation of four generations of family history: pieces of the good dinner service, chairs with tattered upholstery and tobacco stains, moth-eaten rugs and, behind it all, the chest that Juliane had brought with her from Germany on the cart. It must have weighed over 150 kilos, and was an enormous piece of furniture that would not fit into any living room today. Ornate, with heavy-handed swirls, this had contained her every valuable possession. This was our history.

When it was time to leave, a V of swans flew west across the fjord from the Baltic. 'I hope they are not too early,' said Inge. 'There'll be frost again before the spring settles in.' She had been watching them from this window most of her life and seemed confident of their survival after she and her husband had gone. Inge and Halle were leaving Vejle. They were old and tired and were going to Copenhagen to be closer to their children. After seventy years in the town, they no longer knew anyone and their house was now too big for them.

It was Plato who first taught that, while we might try to pull in the opposite direction, we cannot escape our past and how it will inform our lives. When we return to the river's origins, we must do so with open eyes since the source is not there to be reinterpreted, only understood. The river taught both my parents that healing lies in understanding what came before and knowing what cannot be reversed, only renewed. Once this has been accepted, most wounds can be healed. 'The river obscures conscious thought,' wrote Ackroyd, 'and erases memory . . . like some watery narcotic.' My father was drawn to these banks in search of the childhood that he had never had, wanting to start again with his own children. My mother still looks to these waters to flush out bad blood. For both the river was a symbol of regeneration – a way of cleansing the path for the future, and a reconciliation with the past.

When I returned from visiting the source and crossed the river at Oxford, I drew into my lungs with a deep sense of enjoyment the familiar smell. Even on a Sunday night, people were scurrying across the bridge, ignoring the currents below. I paused a moment and wondered where the water that I had run through my fingers was now.

No matter that it was born in my imagination, I felt that there was a journey shared, a secret hidden in its depths, that I could revisit at will. My family's history had become intelligible to me, even though after all these years there were still things that my mother was not telling me.

When we had talked about her reasons for leaving Denmark, it was as though she heard my questions through a great cloud of pain. My words seemed to open and close in front of her like a great concertina, spanning as they were huge distances in time and emotion, but they were too difficult for her. My words were too bold, too raw, I see that now. When she realised that she did not have to answer me, we sat back down again and neither of us spoke for several minutes.

4

The Proving Ground

Many runners can be happy their entire lives running no faster and no further than they did the week before. It takes a special meditative quality to be able to do this, a quality that attracts deep respect. For others there comes a moment when we want to put ourselves to the test and that means competition. That moment may come with a bet, an untraceable affirmation in the dark: 'I can. This year I am going to run a marathon.'

In the spring of 1999 I was preparing for my university finals. In the haze of an all-night house party, the television flickered silently to itself through the ghostly sweet fog of hand-rolled tobacco. The party was winding down into the peace of another Sunday morning and on the other side of the heavy curtains the bells had started to chime as our neighbours got ready for church. Amidst the wreckage of spilt ashtrays and the curled-up bodies of those recently surrendered to narcotic slumber, the last of us held out for one more hour before the inevitable retreat to bed.

On the television screen, there was an explosion of colour in a view from a helicopter as it swept across Blackheath, revealing an army dressed like cockatoos moving towards an invisible point on the horizon. Logical thought is severely hampered in the terminal hours of any party, but as spliffs and cups of tea were passed around I knew that was what I wanted to do. 'I am going to run the London Marathon.' After my outrageous declaration a bet was made and quickly forgotten, but twelve months later I was standing on the start line in Blackheath, wrapped in a bin liner against the cool morning – one of the 35,000.

It was in a similar moment of clarity that, in 1894, an ambitious minor French baron, Pierre de Coubertin, founded the International Olympic Committee at a ceremony at the Sorbonne University in Paris. He raised a glass to 'the Olympic idea, which has traversed the mists of the ages like an all-powerful ray of sunlight and returned to illuminate the threshold of the twentieth century with a gleam of joyous hope'.

In 1889 he had been commissioned by the French government to report on the state of physical education in the national school system. Coubertin, though, had grander ideas than simply stopping French schoolchildren from getting fat, but few were convinced that it would amount to anything and his Olympic announcement was greeted with little enthusiasm.

Coubertin was an unreconstructed Victorian for

whom education was the keystone of society, and sport provided the moral fibre for making men great. While the inspiration for the revival of the Olympics might have come out of the dust of Arcadia, where the Temple of Zeus had presided over the Games for more than a millennium, even before a starting gun had been fired it was clear that Coubertin had appropriated the Olympic ideal for a very different end to that envisaged in Ancient Greece.

Like many French people at the turn of the twentieth century, Coubertin was obsessed with the idea of making France great again after the humiliating defeat in the 1870 Franco-Prussian War. His knowledge of the ancient Olympic Games came less from classical texts than from Germany, whose archaeologists had been commissioned by Kaiser Wilhelm Friedrich IV to excavate the site of Olympia. 'Germany has exhumed what remains of Olympia,' Coubertin declared. 'Why should not France be able to reconstitute its splendour?'

His definition of the Olympic spirit had four principles. The Games were to be treated as a religion. The participants were to 'adhere to an ideal of a higher life, to strive for perfection'; to represent an elite 'whose origins are completely egalitarian' and at the same time uphold the qualities of chivalry with all 'its moral qualities'; to create a truce, a 'four-yearly festival of the springtime of mankind'; and to glorify beauty by the 'involvement of the philosophic act of the Games'.

By the turn of the twentieth century the English Amateur Athletics Club had been growing for over twenty years, and they refused to move beyond the rigid definition of an amateur athlete as 'a person who has never competed in open competition, or for public money . . . or is a *mechanic, artisan* or *labourer*' (italics added). The very idea of a competition for money or involving those not of the highest moral fibre was seen as being in immensely bad taste, going against all Victorian morality. It was exactly the sentiment shared by Coubertin, and after over a thousand years of slumber it was this spirit that he would nurture at the inaugural Games in Athens in 1896.

The spirit of the modern Olympic Games was then, in reality, based less on the memories of the glories of Athens than on the attitude to physical education in nineteenth-century Britain, in which winning was a mildly embarrassing conclusion to proceedings and what really mattered was fair play. Coubertin's model for athletic education, *la pédagogie sportive*, was not drawn from the Ancients, but from the Victorian novel *Tom Brown's Schooldays*, which instilled the virtues of 'initiative, daring, decision and the habit of self-reliance and blaming no one but one's self when one stumbles', as taught through a system of punishing self-exertion. Coubertin took the ideals of breeding 'gentlemanly conduct' and adapted them on an international scale, to 'make men' of the new generation of French citizens.

★

The summer that I graduated from university, I flew south to visit a girlfriend, whom I had not seen for seven months. Within two days of my arrival she suggested that I return to England. As the plane taxied away from the departure gate, the Brisbane skyline doused by the rising sun, she had already turned away. I realised that I would never see her again.

I had not repeated my declaration to run the London Marathon to her, but on my arrival at Heathrow I bought a copy of *Runner's World* and detached the perforated entry form for the millennium London Marathon. Outside the world of elite athletes and running clubs, only rudimentary advice can be found on how to train for a marathon. For those starting out, techniques have progressed little from the great second-century physician Galen, who defined some basic exercises for the legs, arms and abdomen in his classical text *How to Stay Healthy*. For muscles he recommended 'controlled' exercises, 'quick' exercises for speed, and 'violent' exercises for strength. I turned the pages of the magazine to find the best shoes to buy.

My first run took place on 30 September and ended within a mile of my leaving the house. I had barely broken into a sweat but splinters of pain were stabbing at my lungs. I walked back home, hanging my head in shame, avoiding all eye contact with passers-by, afraid that they would be laughing at me for being so perfectly dressed for exercise and yet so obviously unfit.

Early on I found a route from my front door that measured a generous 4 miles on the map. By the time my letter of acceptance arrived in November I had added another 2 miles to the route and was getting used to sweating through multiple layers as the cold and dark of autumn set in. Alex, with whom I had hurtled down Daisy Bank at school, had run the New York Marathon in 3:09.07 the year before and said that he would join me. April still seemed like light years away. The only tangible sign of progress in those early months was the accumulation of blisters on my feet, which I took as evidence that I was doing something right, rather than a warning that I needed to invest in some decent socks.

As autumn turned to winter I put my shorts away and out came the hat, gloves and long-sleeved tops to protect me from the elements. I bought a head torch for my evening runs, and would follow the burrowing light that illuminated my glistening face with a pale glow. Deep under thick layers, running head-on into the harsh artificial headlights of people coming home from work, I had the pavements almost to myself. Where were the 35,000 other runners who had been accepted to take part in the London Marathon?

April is the month in which it seems that, like the rats in Albert Camus's *The Plague*, the runners are sent forth to die on the happy streets of every city. At every street corner and pedestrian crossing, unsolicited competition was waiting for me. While they wheezed and waited for the lights to change, bent over clutching their knees, I could not help myself from trying to reel them in, practising what I imagined it would feel like to pass them along the Embankment in the last of the 26.2 miles. In those final weeks of preparation I came to learn the various unspoken rules that exist between marathon runners. Hidden behind sunglasses, the big-game hunters were still out, their arms slack by their sides, and we would exchange glances of impassive acknowledgement. On one of those last runs, I must have been taking myself too seriously as I heard him call only once he had passed me. 'See you in Greenwich!' But it was too late to stop and compare notes.

With a week to go, on Alex's suggestion I stopped running altogether, and slowly my legs returned to normal. After months of waking up exhausted and going to bed shattered, following a routine of running, showering, dressing and undressing around which I configured my day, I could relax and no longer felt as if I was climbing out of bed every morning with a lead coat over my shoulders. Inevitably I worried that I had not run far enough in training, prompted by the chatter in the office as the race weekend approached. 'Are you ready?'

What a question! I had peaked at 60 miles a week, and had drawn great comfort from reading about the great Australian marathon runner Derek Clayton, who had run 200 miles a week for years on his way to the

first sub 2:10 marathon, before falling apart. My calculations made me believe that, at the speed he was running,
we were spending almost the same amount of time
training each week. On the Saturday morning before
the race I joined the queue to collect my race number
and I laid out my running clothes one last time. I checked
my shoes repeatedly to be sure that the laces were firm
and spent the evening sitting up in bed, flexing my
muscles under the soft, uneven tan line that had appeared
on my legs and arms in the last month.

The start to any marathon is an emotional anticlimax.
Runners move forward hesitantly and come together
without any noticeable antagonism. There is chatter and
posturing, false modesty and nerves, and the smell of
Vaseline and shampoo. For all that, there is not even a
line in the road to indicate the moment at which we
have started the race, but within a mile we are at full
speed and the sweat is starting to prickle over our temples.
By lunchtime it would all be over.

After nearly three millennia the myth of Olympia still
pervades the ruins. By the time Coubertin had resur-
rected the Olympic dream, the site had been lost under
more than 1,000 years of earthquakes and landslides. The
first proposals for excavation were made in 1723 by
Bernard de Montfaucon, a French Benedictine monk.
In 1766, Richard Chandler, a British antiquarian, noticed
Greek farmers ploughing up marble fragments on the

Peloponnese peninsula. What Chandler found amongst the weeds and the algae were the remains of the looted Temple of Zeus, standing in a stagnant pool surrounded by half-tumbled down pillars and walls: a scene of stony desolation, home only to a cloud of gnats. Once the site had been abandoned by Chandler, excavation did not begin in earnest for another 100 years, under the direction of Germany's Kaiser Wilhelm. It was not, however, until a personal commission was granted by Hitler that the site was fully unearthed, in time for the 1936 Berlin Olympics, as he fantasised about uncovering an ancient Aryan paradise.

The site of Olympia lies at the fringes of Arcadia, a mountainous area of the central Peloponnese idealised in the European tradition as the semi-mythical home of pastoral ease, a byword for nymphs and shepherds at play in an enclave of shameless simplicity. The river Alpheus still runs behind what would have been the Gymnasium. To the north stands the pine forest where Zeus, the most awesome and invincible of powers, had wrestled his father, the Titan Kronos, for control of the world.

What Chandler had dusted off was the hidden playground of the ancestors of every athlete that has ever lived and, by extension, anyone who has ever laced up a pair of trainers. Until the excavation, the history of the Olympics had existed only through fragments of Greek, Latin and Arabic text, which merely served to encourage the myth of its divine status. Although archaeologists believe Olympia to have been, from 1100 BC, a religious site dedicated to the earth goddess, Gaea, it was at the first recorded Olympiad, in 776 BC, that Apollo had beaten Hermes in a foot race. Since then, hundreds of thousands of people had come to this site to compete or to worship their heroes.

The civilisation that had conceived the Olympics also gave birth to the gymnasiums of Plato and Aristotle, places that tutored the mind and the body, pushing back the limits of physical capacity, intellectual learning and moral understanding. Ancient Egyptians and Babylonians had been examining the cosmos for generations, but it was not until the coming of Pythagoras, born in 570 BC, that scientific examination and the application of a systematic process of thought based on observation was transposed to the intellectual world. The Greeks came to understand that, to reach their optimum, they must apply the same rigorous processes to their pursuit of intellectual and physical excellence.

It was no coincidence that these gymnasiums adjoined the academies where students learnt of Socrates, Pythagoras and Euclid. The gymnasium was a place to retreat to from the demands of the day and to address the Socratic issues that would have been as refreshing to the mind as cold water to aching limbs. How can we be good? What can we know? The answers to these moral and epistemological questions were inextricably linked to how the Ancient Greeks treated the body. To be the best one could be was a physical as well as an intellectual challenge. For those who trained, manly virtue, or *arête*, was intrinsically bound up with athletic prowess. The athlete's body was the outward form of the virtuous individual, and there was no greater theatre for it than the Olympics. And while the Games were the preserve of the elite, the words from Homer's *Odyssey* – 'There is no greater glory for any man alive than that which he wins by his hands and feet' – were at the core of every Hellenic education. It was here in the gymnasium that athletes would start their ten-month training programme for the Olympics.

Although a fine body does not guarantee a fine mind, well-exercised athletes became the subject of erotic and aesthetic interest, coming to shape the classical definition of *kalokagathia* – beautiful goodness. While Coubertin quietly ignored the very idea of men brought together to practise *gymnazesthai*, literally to exercise naked, he would have understood this environment as a place of ease and recreation. As it was for Coubertin, an artful pugilist, so too for Socrates, who saw that it was only in testing body and mind that the moral fibre of his students could be properly formed. The Secretary General of the inaugural modern Games understood this connection well, claiming that Coubertin's Games, like the Ancients', was 'founded on the same eternal principle . . . for the appreciation of the moral and physical improvement of all free citizens'.

The first recorded Olympics had one event – a 210-yard sprint – and it was won by a cook named Koroibos. For the first thirteen Olympiads, running was the only sport, and over the coming years races of a double lap and then twenty-four laps, roughly 3 miles, were established. Forty thousand spectators would come and watch their favourite athletes toe a line in the sand.

There were no prizes for second place. The shame of defeat drove some men to madness and others to suicide, as it would do in the twentieth century. In 1968, four years after winning the bronze medal in the Tokyo Olympic Marathon in front of his Emperor, Kokichi Tsuburaya followed the samurai tradition of jisatsu. The note he left said simply: 'Sorry; cannot run any more.'

It was this possibility of failure on the one hand and immortality on the other that has dominated the physical and mental ambitions of every athlete. As in our own time, preparation and training take years of patience. While, from our sofas, we keep our eyes on the front of the field at every Olympic Marathon, at the back linger the ghosts of former greats, along with the wide-eyed novices who know that this will not be their time. Whether the training takes 4 years or the ten months originally allocated, the maxim of the Ancients still holds true. 'You say you want to be an Olympic champion. But wait. Think about what is involved . . . You will have to hand your body over to your coach just as you would to a doctor. You will have to obey every instruction.' So wrote the first-century Stoic, Epictetus.

The reward for the winners was unquantifiable compared to the hardship involved. When a runner named Exainetos won a second successive victory in the stadium at the ninety-second Olympics in 412 BC, his native city of Akragas in Sicily presented him with an escort of 300 chariots pulled by white horses. A section of the city wall was knocked down for the hero's entrance. After all, what did a city need walls for, when it had legions of young men like Exainetos?

Even the ordinarily sober Aristotle was overcome as he gazed, spellbound, at the alchemy of the athletes as they transformed flesh and blood into gold. 'In a young man, beauty consists in having a body that can endure all sorts of exertion in running . . . and one that is delightful to gaze upon . . . for men in their prime, beauty belongs to those prepared for the toils of active service: such types are good-looking and awe-inspiring at the same time.'

These athletes were both gods and mortals, worshipped for their physical perfection and adored for the aesthetic quality of their endeavour. For both the athlete and the enraptured spectator, the very act of running had a transformative power, and the winners were seen to be no longer governed either by the laws of gravity or by physical boundaries. Even Pindar, not usually prone to hyperbole, knew what the importance of victory in the Games meant:

> What is man but a short-lived creature? He is but
> the dream of a shadow.
> But when a ray of sunshine comes as a gift from the
> gods –
> A brilliant light settles on mortals, and a gentle life.

It is easy to see how these races sent spectators into raptures. For those watching, victory represented a kind of transcendental grace since their lives were, for the most part, defined by extreme hardship and strife. The obsession with the Games completely mystified non-Greeks. 'What sort of men have you brought us to fight?' a Persian general asked King Xerxes at the height of the invasion of Greece in 480 BC. The Greek soldiers were busy watching the wrestling.

By AD 393 when, from Constantinople, Emperor Theodosius I handed down the edict banning the Olympics on the grounds that it was a pagan festival, competitors were arriving for the Games from the furthest reaches of the Mediterranean, the remotest corners of the civilised world. So deeply ingrained in the culture of the empire had the Games become that when Rome adopted them as its own, it was common to see athletes training by running for an entire day around the perimeter of the Circus Maximus, sometimes covering 150 miles without a break. There is even a legend of one eight-year-old boy who, it is said, ran 70 miles around the chariot racing track in one afternoon.

The edict directly outlawed sacrifice – an integral part of the Olympic festival – a dictum that was first ignored by local priests and then enforced with the death penalty. The view that the Olympics was a sinister carnival of flesh was inevitably renewed by Protestant priests at the Amsterdam Olympics in 1928 who advised their flock to stay away, a request they happily disobeyed. In AD 426, Theodosius II ordered the demolition of all existing pagan temples, with the decree that the Temple of Jupiter be burnt to the ground. This brought to an end over a thousand years of aesthetic spectacles, coupled with an orgy of flesh, wine, dizzying athletic achievement and myth-making.

Emboldened by the length of Christianity's reach in the fourth century, Ambrose of Milan, the city's thin-lipped bishop, declared the Olympics heretical since the Games contravened the Nicene Creed. For one of the founding doctors of the Church, the Word was made flesh, not the other way around. His strict piety, emphasising the intellectual contemplation of God, chimed with popular complaints about the narcissism of the Games and an increasing squeamishness about nudity in public. But Ambrose's warnings from the heavens were too late. The values of physical culture articulated in classical Greece had become a part of the medieval world. Sport, even serious sport, was fun. People understood it as a diversion, an escape from the drudgery of work and mere survival, and it gave subjugated communities across the continent the opportunity to claim back a part of their lives from their masters.

Before the Olympic torch became an eternal flame, it smouldered back to life sporadically in the seventeenth century with some rustic jamborees in the West Country of Britain. The Greeks too had rather miserably tried and failed to revive the 4-year cycle in 1859 and again in 1870, by which time athletics could be witnessed throughout Britain at more than six purpose-built running tracks. By the turn of the twentieth century, the precursors to the Tour de France, which began in 1903, were taking place across the Channel. The first Bordeaux–Paris cycling race covered a 358-mile course, won in 26 hours and 35 minutes in 1891, 'which saw the sun go down over the plains of Poitou, and rise over the forest of Rambouillet'. In the Paris–Brest–Paris race in September of the same year, cyclists, bent double over their steel frames, pedalled furiously through the Normandy countryside where villagers had set up tables laden with milk, apples, cider and cakes, all of which the contestants devoured at speed. It is a tradition upheld by today's Paris Marathon where runners are offered oysters, foie gras and red wine as they pass along the banks of the Seine.

It seems inevitable that Coubertin's Olympics should have included a race that commemorated an event that never took place. The bare facts of Pheidippides' feat are so limited that they are open to minimal interpretation, but, along with forty-two other events across nine sports, Coubertin was persuaded by his friend Michel Bréal to offer 'a fine silver cup' for a race to celebrate 'the famous run of the Marathon soldier', Pheidippides.

Fourteen nations took part in the Games of 1896, financed and organised by their Athenian hosts, which brought together the best amateur athletes. In the introduction to the official report of the Games, Timoleon Philemon, the Secretary General, wrote that Olympia had assembled 'the flower of civilised humanity . . . in order to bear witness to the continuous development and improvement, both intellectual and physical, of those who were the rulers, the inhabitants, and the defenders of cities'. Carefully ignoring elements of the ancient Olympics, such as the ever-present stench of the sacrificed carcasses or the chaos of sweating bodies and drunken revelry, he instead concentrated on the idea that those historic Games prefigured 'the rise of that more general doctrine of the brotherhood and peaceful union of all nations dwelling upon earth', convinced that it was 'a step towards the grand idea of "united humanity"'.

The architectural centrepiece of Coubertin's Games was the reconstructed Panathenaikon stadium, which had originally been built in 330 BC and today forms the last gasping 100 metres of the Athens Marathon. From the track the tiered stone seats soar up into the Mediterranean sky. On the morning of the Olympic Marathon, a full house of nearly 72,000 took their seats alongside the king of Greece, in desperation rather than expectation. The hosts had had a miserable Games until that morning, with not a single gold in a track and field event, and a solitary champion in the fencing. On Saturday 10 April, seventeen runners made their way out along the undulating road to the race start at Marathon. Today the road is tarmacked, and those who come to run the Athens Marathon are driven to have their photo taken near the waist-high obelisk by the side of the road, commemorating the start of Coubertin's Marathon.

When I arrived in Athens to run the marathon, my geography had taught me to expect a flat race between two coastal points. As we were bussed out of the city, the sun rose over two ranges of hills, both of which we had to cross. Starting at 25 metres above sea level, the course drops down swiftly, before rising 80 metres over the next 10 kilometres. The second hill, I could see now, came between 15 and 30 kilometres, rising to 220 metres before the final spine-shattering descent into Athens. I had laughed at the announcer on the start line when he chided the elite who had not come to Greece because it was too difficult a course. 'You are all heroes!' we were told. In truth the reason why there were so few top athletes here was that there is more money and prestige in New York, where they were hosting their marathon the following weekend.

At the inaugural Games, the Australian Teddy Flack, who worked in London and trained on the Commons at Wimbledon and Barnes, was going for a third gold medal to complement his victory in the 800 and 1,500 metres. Somewhere in the middle of the pack was Spiridon Louis, aged twenty-three, from nearby Maroussi, who had qualified in a time of 3:18.27, and who had been convinced days earlier by Colonel Papadiamantopoulos, the official starter, to take part.

The race was classic in its amateurishness. Flack had enlisted the butler from the British embassy to ride with him on a bicycle; and the competitors had been declared fit by doctors who had tested their reflexes by tapping their knees with a hammer. The runners assembled at the start line like a gathering of football fans at the stadium gates, in a wardrobe of singlets, buttoned shirts and cloth caps, accompanied by Greek soldiers on horseback, offering beer and milk to help them stay hydrated.

Most of the seventeen runners bolted as the gun went off. The French 1,500-metres silver medallist, Albin Lermusiaux, wearing white gloves in honour of the king

of Greece, disappeared over the horizon almost immediately. Apart from the qualifying race that they had all
taken part in, not a single runner had competitive experience of running for more than the time it took to
complete the 1,500 metres.

At the 15-kilometre mark, covered in 52 minutes,
Lermusiaux was 3 kilometres ahead of his nearest rival,
while Spiridon was busy being fortified by a flask of
wine and a hard-boiled egg handed to him by his step-
father. Most of the runners made the same mistakes that
I would later make and started to fall away during the
second steep climb. Flack steadily gained on the leaders,
apparently running the perfect race. Spiridon was now
more than 6 minutes down, a massive distance to make
up, even over the course of a marathon.

On the plane to Athens there had been an entire dele-
gation of runners, but I had avoided them by keeping
my hood up and my eyes on the floor. After all, I was
competing against them. Across the aisle sat two of them.
One, older than me by at least fifteen years, kept checking
his gold watch and the laces on his trainers. His fore-
arms were thick with hair, but his everyday ordinariness was belied by muscles that told of thousands of
miles run in the sun. I could beat him, though.

I did not see him in the hotel, or when I registered,
but 10 kilometres into the race he appeared at my left
shoulder, easy to spot in his orange vest, his body leaner

and more compact than I had noticed on the plane. His cap came off and he doused himself in water, momentarily slowing, before striding out ahead of me. I would catch him on the hill, I told myself. But by halfway I was already slowing – I could not understand where these mountains had come from. I had fallen apart in many previous marathons from lack of training, but here I was boiling up, with the sun searing my skin.

At the fulcrum of the race, Spiridon materialised on Flack's shoulder, looking 'very fresh and running well', according to the race report, and they ran through the 38 kilometres mark together. There is a distant comfort in knowing that the descent into Athens has broken greater runners than me. It was here, at the 2004 Athens Olympics, that Paula Radcliffe could no longer withstand the forces consuming her from within. It was here too that Flack's own race came to an end, leaving Spiridon, now refreshed by some orange slices given to him by the girl he would later marry, alone out front and virtually the only runner left.

As Spiridon pounded down the hill towards the stadium, Colonel Papadiamantopoulos appeared beside him on his white horse to hand him some cognac, before racing off, kicking up the dust, to tell the waiting Greek royal family the news that they had hoped for. 'Hellene, Hellene!' the crowd echoed when they realised what was going on – a Greek! Covered in 25 miles of dust and sweat, the bloodied runner in vest number 17 was greeted as though he had descended from Mount Olympus. The myth of Pheidippides had been made flesh. 'Rejoice! We conquer!' His time of 2:58.50 was 7 minutes – over a mile – up on the nearest competitor, another Greek.

Once Spiridon had been crowned, having turned down the offer of free meals for life and a plot of land, and accepting only a horse and cart to replace his donkey, rumours started to congeal amongst the foreign visitors. Before Flack had been reduced to a standstill, his butler had turned around to see how far back the other runners were. Flack was told that the race was his to lose, but within a mile Spiridon had appeared. Spiridon had never run competitively at any distance before and he would never run again. Many, including Norris McWhirter of *The Guinness Book of Records*, were of the opinion that Spiridon had hitched a ride on horseback from one of the Greek soldiers. He knew the terrain around Marathon well, and over the coming years villagers who had grown up with him gossiped that he had taken a short cut through the forest to make up the ground on Flack. However, Spiridon never confessed. Flack kept his counsel, considering it ungentlemanly to question his host's triumph.

Spiridon returned to an Olympic stadium only once, at the invitation of Hitler, to carry the flag of his nation at the 1936 Olympics before the Führer presented him with an olive branch, claimed to have been cut from the sacred grove of Zeus at Olympia itself.

★

Within six months of the Olympic Games, Bréal's modest proposal had been brought to Boston, and the oldest public marathon was founded. It gave ordinary people the chance to line up with the country's finest athletes on level terms.

London won the bid to host the 1908 Olympics and, just as Athens had, they hosted the marathon as one of the final events, to attract natural middle-distance runners to a race that few had run, let alone trained specifically for. Spectators, journalists and the athletes themselves all understood that it was the greatest physical and mental challenge in the Olympic schedule. The day that the starting gun went off, *The Times* wrote: 'Besides the marathon all other events, which momentarily interest, pale into insignificance.' Winning the 100-metre or even 1,500-metre race was primarily about bloodlines – having the good fortune to be built faster than the rest. The marathon was a psychological test and even in its short history it had not been won by the fastest, but by the smartest runner.

When the schedule had been drawn up, the London Olympic committee planned the same 25-mile distance that Spiridon had run, starting in Windsor and mapping the course along the river east to the stadium at White City. However, days before the race, the Princess of Wales requested that the start be moved to the grounds of Windsor Castle, under the windows of the royal nursery, so that her children could enjoy the spectacle, as they could not possibly get to the royal box in the stadium to join the king in time for the finish. Her request was granted adding an extra 1 mile and 385 yards of incalculable cruelty for exhausted athletes. Everyone who has run the course of the London Marathon remembers most vividly the last miles that turn off the Embankment at Westminster to Birdcage Walk and the final turn down the Mall. I have now run this course three times and although the flag at Buckingham Palace has not been flying, I like to think that Her Majesty was there at the window, watching our last strides, for if it was not for her family we would already be sitting on the pavement with a cup of tea and a biscuit.

The added mile and a bit had a more dramatic implication for Italy's long-distance champion, Dorando Pietri, a baker from Capri who had won the 25-mile Paris Marathon the year before. With 50 yards to go, far out in the lead, he collapsed, rose, 'burst into a horrible parody (almost pathetic) of spurts', according to *The Times*, then dropped again 10 yards from the tape. With the support of the race officials, he staggered forward and reached the line, only to be disqualified.

The officials later protested that they had no choice but to help Pietri since it 'was not right that people should have to watch this suffering'. Yet it was through the suffering that the crowd had found a hero, the queen herself awarding him a special trophy. According to the

Times editorial: 'Her woman's heart had prompted her to mark the sympathy which, in common with all who saw the tragic finish of the race, she felt for his pluck and his disappointment.' Sir Arthur Conan Doyle, who was at the finish line, later wrote: 'I think in that assembly not any man would have wished to see victory torn at that instant from the plucky little Italian . . . it is horrible, yet fascinating, this struggle between a set purpose and an utterly exhausted frame.'

For the press, the reality of what a marathon felt like to run had caught up with the myth. No longer was it an adventurous pursuit: it was as real as flesh and bone, and had the capacity to destroy individuals. For weeks after, there was speculation as to whether the marathon would ever be staged again, since those present agreed that Pietri's condition after the race had been worse than that of a prize-fighter after a knockout blow. The debate was revived four years later, in Stockholm, when the marathon killed its first runner, the Portuguese Francisco Lázaro, who burnt up with dehydration, having inexplicably coated himself in wax to prevent sweating, leading to severe body fluid electrolyte imbalance.

The work ethic of the athlete was dictated for decades to come by the Amateur Athletic code, drawn up in the nineteenth century. Numerous runners were disqualified, including Paavo Nurmi, who was banned from the 1932 Olympics for having received either cash prizes or silverware that was deemed to be of too high a value for him to remain classed as an amateur. Similarly, it was frowned upon to train too much. When, in 1952, Emil Zátopek thrashed his body to three gold medals in eight days on a training programme of 100 miles a week, the running establishment looked on in disapproval. That was not how things were done. It was the first time in the modern Games that anyone had won gold in the 5,000 metres, the 10,000 metres and the marathon, setting Olympic records in each race. He was also the first person since Leonidas of Rhodes, in 164 BC, to win the gold medal in all three distance footraces at the same Olympic Games.

The wounded Roger Bannister condemned Zátopek's achievements as 'sub-human', effectively accusing him of cheating by training so hard, since it did not give others a chance. Those who had upheld the nature of amateurism were as disconnected from the reality that had created the myths of Olympia as Coubertin had been sixty years earlier. For them it was enough to cover a few laps of the track briskly. They had lost sight of the staggering amount of hard work that had crafted the bodies of the athletes of Ancient Greece.

Footage of the 1952 Olympics holds only some of the clues to how Emil Zátopek took a sport, dominated by the straitjacket approach of the amateur elite, and presented it to the world in a fashion that required a completely new vocabulary. He seemed to climb through the air in slow motion, his arms reaching out to drag himself forward, on his way to his second gold medal in the 10,000 metres. Zátopek understood that the only way to significantly improve was to push himself further and further out of his comfort zone. This he achieved by spending hours alone, perfecting a technique of interval training around the running track near his home in Moravia, Czechoslovakia, getting a profound and addictive pleasure from the fatigue resulting from running up to 20 miles a day.

For long-distance athletes, there is before Zátopek and after Zátopek. Fred Wilt, author of *How They Train*, puts these mammoth daily sessions into their historical context. 'Before Zátopek, nobody realised it was humanly possible to train this hard. Emil is truly the originator of modern intensive training.' Between May 1948 and July 1954 he won thirty-eight consecutive 10,000-metre races.

He entered his first competitive race over 1,500 metres at the age of twenty and came fourth out of five, but for Zátopek the experience was a matter of learning, not winning. He resolved every problem through scientific application, coupled with an almost childlike curiosity, although he had been told his attempt was futile since, with none of the grace of his competitors, he would never win. He tested his ideas and studied the results as if posing a series of conjectures and refutations, until he found a formula that visibly improved his time, speed and strength. By the end of the year he was running 36 kilometres a day, while the British indulged themselves with memories of victories that would be celebrated in *Chariots of Fire*.

His racing style of 'thrashing, churning, agonising, grimacing', in the words of one of his competitors, the American Johnny Kelly Jnr, derived from a complete reinvention of how to train. 'Why should I practise running slowly? I already know how to run slow. I must learn to run fast,' he would say to uncomprehending journalists, who saw Zátopek only on race day, his elbows wide, his head tilted, pulling away from the pack in a wild sprint that seemed to explode out of his exhausted body.

Round and round he would go: 100 metres fast, 100 slow, over and over again, watched in bemusement by his club mates. In winter he would train through the forests in his army boots and, when he changed into his running shoes – whoosh! When it was too cold even to run outside, he would put the washing into the bath and, wearing his army boots, pound away for hours until soapsuds flowed down the hallway.

He called it the training of willpower. Perhaps because he was not the most naturally gifted of athletes – his movements were too jagged for purists – he compensated with an inexorable determination to keep improving, doing what the next man was not willing to endure. 'By keeping and increasing his exercise a person can train his willpower. Then when he races he can force himself to give a better performance. You can really train your will . . . you can do anything in your power,' he observed years later. As an abstraction, training the willpower was about self-discipline. 'When a person trains once, nothing happens. When a person forces himself to do a thing 100 times then he certainly has developed. Is it raining? That doesn't matter. Am I tired? That doesn't matter either. Then willpower is no longer a problem.'

It was an attitude recognised by the Soviet reporters at the 1948 London Olympics. In an effort to encourage factory workers to pledge higher outputs, Zátopek's gold in the 10,000 metres was held up to show all good communists that 'the moral strength of great, human record reaches far beyond itself'. His aim was to train until his body was broken, sometimes leaving him vomiting by the side of the track, a proposition that would have appalled the English school of runners.

Zátopek arrived in Helsinki on 11 July 1952, having caught a cold while cross-country running in the spring, which meant that he had hardly run at all in the final months of preparation. He went straight to the track from the airport, eager to make up for lost time.

As Zátopek was the defending Olympic 10,000-metre champion, his name was known to some. However, even to those who knew him from having successfully defended his title and won gold in the 5,000 metres, his decision to run the marathon came as a surprise, since he had not trained for it and it would be his third event in eight days.

At the halfway mark he was out in front with the British favourite, Jim Peters, and turned to him, saying, 'I know virtually nothing about marathon running, but don't you think we ought to go a little faster?' Peters shook his head as Zátopek broke away. At 25 kilometres, Zátopek declined the offer of lemonade, assuming that he had to pay for it, and he began to ache, the pain of his weakening body etched deeply in the lines on his face. At 35 kilometres, Peters retired with cramp, leaving Zátopek on his own, his head rolled to one side, like Paula Radcliffe's in her final kick, arms clawing across his chest, his expression fixed in anguish. He wanted to quit. Blood was filling his shoes as his toenails popped but he could see the Olympic flame. 'I decided I must run to the flame.'

He ran as if he had been stabbed in the heart, it was said. 'Zá-to-pek! Zá-to-pek!' the crowd screamed. When he crossed the finish line, more dead than alive, people said, a Czech journalist was already filing his piece on Zátopek as a true communist hero. 'Zátopek's name has become synonymous with tenacity, effort, reliability and willpower. Zátopek's industrious conscientiousness, bravery and responsibility should enter all our lives.' The Finnish crowned him 'Satu-Pekka' – the legendary Peter.

Zátopek taught athletes that success – real success that

broke records and bodies, and redefined the way that spectators engaged with the runner – required running on the outer margins of human endurance.

Watching Zátopek that afternoon was the Swedish coach of the Ethiopian national running team, Onni Niskanen. Niskanen had grown up with distance running. For the Finns and the Swedes the marathon distance had a special significance beyond simple sporting achievement, offering a metaphor for the vast emptiness of the Nordic landscape and man's frailty when faced with traversing even an infinitesimal part of it. It was a sport requiring a monumental exertion that defied nature. Zátopek's ability to transcend perceived human limits was not about becoming superhuman, as incredulous spectators cried, their hands clutched to their foreheads. Rather, Zátopek had shown that running could make them feel more acutely human, not because they were conquering the great outdoors by strengthening themselves against it, but by becoming one with it.

Niskanen had been sent to the Helsinki Olympics at the request of Emperor Selassie, who wanted his country to compete on the great Olympic stage, having been insultingly told, after Ethiopia's application for the Amsterdam Olympics of 1928, that Africans were not ready to take part in international sporting events – 'Les Africains doivent pratiquer le sport dans leur pays d'abord pour le comprendre.' Niskanen brought Zátopek's interval training back to Addis Ababa and started to apply it to his runners. In return for the promise that he would bring the emperor an Olympic medal, he got permission to take the best Ethiopian athletes to Sweden to test them on a treadmill, the first that they had ever seen. It was a cold, brutal machine – regulated, statistical and infallible – that pitted the body not against a rival or even against nature, but against hard science.

The series of tests revealed that the Ethiopians were unlike any European runners who had undergone the same examinations. For a start, they hardly sweated. It was as if they were able to conserve water deep in their tissue. The machine showed that Niskanen's runners were physiologically not sprinters, since they lacked the power and danger that comes with bulk physical muscle, ready to explode with the energy waiting within. Instead, it appeared that his runners had an innate capacity to cover very long distances. If they could only learn how to relax their breathing, run with their bodies upright, up on their toes rather than flat-footed, they would be able to compete at the highest level.

Abebe Bikila, a private in the emperor's guard, was one of Niskanen's athletes, and it was immediately clear that he was not a sprinter since his hip carriage was too high. He was all legs. When his torso loosened, they would reach forward, pulling him along effortlessly. He even held his elbows in tightly at his waist without having to be told to. Where those unfamiliar with the sport saw fluidity, other athletes saw pure geometry. He ran like a stone skipping across the surface of a lake.

For the 1960 Olympics in Rome, Abebe Wakgira was chosen for the marathon ahead of Bikila. He had repeatedly broken Zátopek's Olympic record and at thirty-seven was facing his last chance. Bikila was to stay behind to keep training for the nationals until Wami Biratu, who was the second member of the marathon team, before whom other runners had cowered, broke his ankle playing football. Suddenly Bikila was on the plane.

Few Europeans had seen the Ethiopians run before, and the marathon that year was thick with political overtones. The race started in the shadow of the Colosseum and of the monoliths stolen from Ethiopia, and it finished at the Arch of Constantine, where Mussolini's troops had set off to conquer Ethiopia twenty-five years earlier. It was left to the journalists to pen the metaphors, but the emperor made much of the significance of the Games as a political statement, a chance to take back something from the country whose invasion of his own had defined a generation.

There was great expectation on the cycling team, but they failed even to qualify for the finals. Bikila, who was no political animal, had just been told the story of Pheidippides and at first was more concerned with the possibility that he would die in the effort if he won. Niskanen calmed him by putting the race in perspective. 'It is not like other races. The distance runner is not like other runners. He can't see the finish line. When he begins the race, he doesn't even know if he going to reach the end.' Bikila knew then that he could complete it. He knew that he could run all day if asked, but he was having trouble with his running shoes and asked permission to run barefoot.

He ran the way he always ran, unaware of the gladiatorial setting or the fuss people were making over his bare feet. Once the runners had made it past the crowds at the start line, which officials had trouble holding back, his heightened senses were free to take in the smells of wild sage and pink laurel.

Bikila was a perfect athlete and his tactic was simply never to be in a hurry. Unlike Zátopek, who ran more like a boxer by comparison, Bikila drifted through the field like the wind, hardly noticed by those around him, moving up without any sense of haste. It made the other athletes feel as though they were simply succumbing to the natural order of things, rather than being overtaken. It was not until he passed the Piazza di Porta, with only Rhadi Ben Abdesselam, the Moroccan favourite, with him that his style changed and he dipped his shoulders for the finish line.

Bikila broke Zátopek's record by 7:47 minutes in what could be described as the best marathon race ever. He had lost 300 grams in the 2 hours, and finished with the words, 'Twenty-six miles is nothing to me.' There was none of Zátopek's anguish that made the crowds feel as though they could empathise with his pain. His victory was born out of a natural ability that had been hidden from view only because of the political view that the African continent was not developed enough. The marathon distance had found its athlete.

Four years later, in Tokyo, in front of Zátopek and Jesse Owens and 100,000 spectators, he did it again. Like Zátopek in 1952, he had been released from hospital a matter of mere weeks before — after an operation on his appendix — and put 4 minutes between himself and the British competitor Basil Heatley. He crossed the finish line and stretched. No runner had successfully defended his Olympic record, either before or since, and Bikila gave his medal to the doctor who had operated on him.

Four years on from Tokyo he arrived in Mexico, again the favourite, but pulled up with the leg injury of an ageing athlete and instructed his fellow Ethiopian, Mamo Wolde, to win. 'Sir! Yes, sir!' Wolde replied. The Olympic Marathon gold was presented to the emperor for the third and last time, before he was overthrown and imprisoned. Bikila retired with the words, 'Once I was a child, I could not walk. But then I learned to walk. Then I became a boy. And I learned to run.'

By the 1970s science had started to teach runners and coaches about the chemical transformations that the body undergoes during exercise. Until then, from Galen's second-century advice through to Niskanen's programme, every training manual had been based on the immediately observable world. Now coaches were able to look through a microscope at the blood of the perfect athlete.

Bikila's encounter with the first primitive running machine was the closest his generation came to the modernity that we take for granted every time we step inside a health club. By the time the great names of the modern era – David Bedford, Brendan Foster and Ron Hill – were competing, top athletes had already spent a decade examining what happens to the body as a result of running 200 miles a week.

As the crowds gather at the start line of any marathon, it is easy to distinguish those who are there to race from those who are there just to take part. Vacuum-packed sachets of glucose gel are gripped tightly and bottles of sports drinks in an array of medicine-cabinet colours are consumed as we amateur runners copy the professionals in their final preparations. Although my running shoes had been named to suggest that they had been scientifically engineered at the CERN Hadron Collider, it is in these mouthfuls of sugary relief that the science of running has benefited the masses. Torn sachets litter every checkpoint, and those who slow to a crushing walk are inevitably those who did not come fully prepared. While few of the runners are genuine athletes, the invention of these globules of energy allow us all, for the morning, to behave like our heroes.

What Bikila knew intuitively when he said that he could run all day was later proved by scientific papers that showed that East African runners had a much greater resistance to fatigue than other athletes. And it is something close to this that we aspire to when we take on the marathon. During repeated muscle contractions, East Africans outperformed European and American runners with VO2 max capacities of 89 per cent compared to 81 per cent. In real terms they are able to sustain higher levels of skeletal recruitment before developing fatigue. They are also shorter and considerably lighter – up to 14 kilos – as well as being constituted of a different ratio of muscle fibre, conducive to endurance training.

The Rift Valley, which runs at altitude through Ethiopia and Kenya, has produced some of the greatest distance runners of the last thirty years – 45 per cent of the top finishers in all international distances from the 1,500 metres to the marathon. At altitude, with less oxygen the kidneys secrete the hormone erythropoietin (EPO), which stimulates the production of additional, oxygen-carrying blood cells. Breathing under duress at 10,000 feet feels like drinking a milkshake through a thin straw, but by the time the body returns to sea level the lungs billow out with the extra capacity. In a language that would not have been understood even a decade earlier, athletes soon realised that altitude training was worth as much as 3 per cent extra physical capacity. And it was here, in the oxygen-starved air of the Entoto Forest, that Haile Gebreselassie, the greatest distance runner of our generation, came to train when he decided that he too was going to be a runner.

But altitude alone is no great advantage, for Switzerland has yet to produce a top-class distance runner. For Gebreselassie the key is the same paradigm shift that Zátopek had brought about – hard work, organisation, intelligent training and patience. After all, it had taken Mamo Wolde twenty years to achieve his Olympic gold medal.

It was said of Gebreselassie by one of his oldest friends that 'Every Ethiopian feels a call from inside his soul to dream and declare himself free.' Running was a way of unchaining oneself from the political system that had overthrown the oppressive regime of the emperor. The Ethiopian governments that came into power thereafter appreciated that sport was a way of preparing the younger generation for a working life of higher productive labour for the benefit of the wider society and 'the defence of the socialist homeland'. For Gebreselassie it was far more personal. What Bikila had achieved in the Games was to open up long-distance running to a new generation who understood that this sport was for them too.

The seventies was also the decade in which America, if not the world, realised that running was an experience that could be enjoyed by all. Three times in the last century there has been a spike in distance running in America. It happened first during the Great Depression of the 1930s when more than 200 runners set the trend by racing 40 miles a day across the continent in what would become the Great American Footrace. Most recently it occurred after 9/11.

When Frank Shorter won the 1972 Munich Olympic Marathon, the country was recovering from the Vietnam War and the race riots. Americans were mesmerised by images on their television screens of events happening far away, transmitted in Technicolor. Holding up his gold medal, Shorter told the world what runners had always known: 'Running is the kind of sport where, once it becomes a part of your daily routine, there's very little attrition.' People didn't have to invest in equipment or join a club. They could dig out an old pair of trainers and run around their local park. No longer was running a sport kept behind the closed perimeter of a fence and reserved for the elite. The explosion in interest that came with Shorter's declaration made runners of even the most unsophisticated athletes.

By the 1980s distance running was so popular that Jimmy Fixx's *The Complete Book of Running* became an instant best-seller around the world. The best runners were starting to become recognised professional athletes who trained all year round, moving from race to race, attracting sponsorships, media coverage and growing audiences. Dick Beardsley, the joint winner of the inaugural London Marathon, was only one of a generation of runners whose lives were recorded on television. Along with Frank Shorter, Bill Rodgers, Alberto Salazar and the tragic Steve Prefontaine, who died before he could win on the greatest stage, the progress of these runners was followed avidly through the year by households across Europe and North America.

It was into this intoxicating climate of enthusiasm, when runners were becoming celebrities, that, in 1979, Chris Brasher returned from New York, having reported on the city's marathon, and posed a challenge. 'Couldn't London stage such an event?' In 1981 he got his race. It was still a curiosity, involving amateur elite runners with only a few thousands on the starting line, but by 1982 the International Association of Athletics Federations allowed sponsorship money to be given out and athletes to turn professional. Within ten years the London Marathon would become the greatest public sporting event ever seen.

The word 'athlete' derives from the Greek *athleo*, meaning to compete for a prize, but it also has its etymology in a word that means 'I struggle, I contest, I suffer'. Pain is hardly the privilege of the elite, and it is the ultimate leveller. If the beauty of the marathon is in part defined by the pain that runners endure, then this is because the marathon offers the possibility of sharing similar states with the elite athletes who inspire us. Regardless of our talent, to have arrived at the start line of a marathon requires strict discipline, a necessary self-regard and focus that excludes all else. The narcissism of the athlete will emerge, as we become runners, when we realise that we are self-creators – engineers of ourselves. What unites the athletes of Ancient Greece, Zátopek and the first-time marathoner is that we have produced a runner from within ourselves through sacrifice and pain, love and care.

Our success as runners, whatever our ability, is defined by how we respond to that pain. The question that spectators behind the barricades along the Embankment ask of every runner is: 'Will they stand up to the pain?' Or as their legs appear to turn to ice, shattering with every step in the last few miles, 'Will they forgo all the hard work and break into a walk?' As Haruki Murakami wrote,

> Pain seems to be a pre-condition to this kind of sport . . . it is precisely because of the pain, precisely because we want to overcome that pain, that we get the feeling, through this process, of really being alive – or at least a partial sense of it. Your quality of experience is based not on standards such as time or ranking, but on finally awakening to an awareness of the fluidity within the action itself. If things go well, that is.

Coubertin would have been horrified by the bastard-isation of his Olympic Marathon, turning it into a public event in which anyone could compete. In truth, however, the modern marathon shares a greater proximity to the aspirations nurtured on the plains of Arcadia than he would have been prepared to admit. The marathon provides us mortals with the nearest thing to Olympic glory that us can hope for, by bringing us face to face with all that defines the athletes' experience. By stripping down to our bare essence, each of us on the start line brings to life the legacy handed down by our ancestors.

I was due to fly out of Athens a few hours after I finished the marathon. On the roof terrace of my hotel I spent as long as I could floating in the freezing November water of the pool, willing the lactic acid to leave my blood and ease the stiffness. The sun was setting through the haze of smog over the hills towards Elefsina whose features were defined only by their jagged monotone edges against the sky. Ahead of me were the Acropolis and the Agora, where John Foden and his team had set off for Sparta, and from where Pheidippides would have run in 490 BC. In less than ten months' time I would be back, standing in the same spot, facing west towards Sparta. I shivered, got dressed and left for the airport.

5

One More Mile, Then I'll Come Home

The night that I stepped up to ultra-distance running, I felt immediately that I was an impostor. Every day for a week I had been watching the weather reports worsen and at the last minute had spent £200 on a 'scientific-ally engineered' Gore-Tex wind- and rain-proof top. I bedded down that night in the way schoolchildren do on the last night of the holidays: with nervous antici-pation of what the day ahead would hold. I looked forward to putting on my new jacket, which I came to see as being the difference between my success and failure on the Round Rotherham, 50-mile-trail, ultra-marathon.

I had found out about the Round Rotherham only six weeks previously when I had gone to interview Rory Coleman, a veteran of nearly 700 marathons and 165 ultra-marathons, with nine Guinness World Records for long-distance running to his name. He invited me into his home and told me his story.

Rory is the best known of the ultra-distance evangelists in the UK. Although I wanted to learn from him as a way of understanding better the psychology of these athletes, I did so as much for my own peace of mind. The decision to take on the Spartathlon had partly come out of the dark, and I wanted to know how much of the desire to take on these challenges comes from within us, driven by specific traits of personality. To run 26.2 miles, I kept being told, was not that difficult. To run all day and all night took something else. But what was that something else? Was it something that you either did or did not have?

Rory had been drunk for nearly ten years. Then, on 5 January 1994, six months after the birth of his son and weighing 15 stone, he put on a pair of plimsolls and ran to the end of the road. By the spring he had lost 3 stone. In April of that year he ran his first half-marathon and had completed his first marathon within twelve months. As many first-timers do, he hit the wall at 20 miles, due to the lactic acid in his muscles and his own inexperience, but he was completely hooked, describing that year of running as the happiest eleven months of his life. He had metamorphosed into a new person, shedding almost every part of his previous self, although it took him another five years to end his unhappy marriage, by which time he had chalked up 100 marathons.

The compulsive behaviour of an alcoholic who first discovers distance running and then, later, finds God does not alone explain why 35,000 people line up, just once, to run a marathon or one of the myriad ultra-distance races around the world.

'If you love something it is easy,' he offered by way of explanation, but by 1995 Rory was running a marathon a week. That his previous life had been deeply unhappy is painfully obvious; however, this was not simply about quitting a forty-a-day smoking habit to lose a bit of weight and get fit. When, in 2004, the BBC found out about Rory and his decision to run 1,275 miles from London to Lisbon – 30 miles a day for forty-three days – the first question was whether there was something obsessive and addictive about his personality that was true of his life both as an alcoholic and as a distance runner. The explicit suggestion was that if he stopped running he would go back to drinking. He shrugs his shoulders, saying that this is not the case. He has been dry now for seventeen years, which he puts down to being focused, able to concentrate on one thing absolutely.

What is clear, though, is that he has an unnaturally hard constitution: the ability present in the likes of Zátopek to do what the next man is not willing to do. The fact that Rory talks of now running three or four marathons a week shows that he has a radically different appreciation of why he runs so far. For the elite, and even for most recreational long-distance runners, the focus is on how to improve on the personal best time.

For those like Rory – and perhaps this is where God fits into his life most comfortably – there is a more holistic understanding of why we run.

In 2004, on his way to Lisbon, he came to see that there was a privilege to the running experience, a kind of spirituality that comes when you have thought about everything there is to think about. For Rory it occurred as he passed through the cornfields of northern Spain. A church bell chimed out the hour and he stopped to marvel at the view. Ten years previously he had been at the bottom of a glass. And now this landscape lent itself to euphoria and rejoicing – an experience of grace to treasure.

'Why do we do this?' he asked. 'Because we have to. There is a deep, visceral need to. It really matters. When you have experienced that euphoria' – a word that he kept coming back to – 'everything else disappears into insignificance.' Medically this is explained by a chemical imbalance of endorphins flooding the bloodstream to hold off the pain. Fell-runners, like Richard Askwith, who described with great eloquence the days – weeks even – of a sense of 'resolution' at the challenge having been accomplished, know that it lasts only as long as it takes for the next challenge to form in the mind. For Rory, though, running was a way of life, a means of becoming a better person, not through pain or competition, but through seeing the world anew and appreciating what he had already achieved. It lies deep within him, of course, but it is also 'out there', he said. And it was knowing that the experience was always waiting for him that made him return to it again and again.

In every sense, for Rory, running is his legacy. 'We are always running towards the horizon,' he told me later, as if he had not explained it well enough already. 'Five miles into a 10-mile run, the horizon is still 5 miles away. But look behind you. Those 5 miles are covered. Whatever happens, no one can take those away from you. That is the difference between how I ran before Lisbon and after. Before I set off, the excitement came with the next run. The challenge had to be bigger and bigger. During those forty-three days en route to Lisbon, I learnt to look over my shoulder, to see where I had come from and put it in context. I learnt to celebrate the achievement.' This was his lesson to me – to honour what you have already accomplished.

Rory now spends as much of his time organising races as he does taking part in them. The evangelist in him wants others to encounter for themselves what he has come to see as an essential part of his daily life. He talked of the letters he has received from people saying how running has changed their lives. Anyone who has waited at the finishing line of any race will have seen the tears of those who finish, emotionally overwhelmed by the experience. For Rory, if you do not cry at such times, then you are not human, and you will not understand the privilege involved in distance running. By contrast, if you are prepared to give every last scintilla of energy, you are ready to take on any distance.

When he talks about his life now, as a trainer and running evangelist, his language is exactly that of a pastor. In answer to questions such as 'Why we are here,' he describes running as an opportunity, for him, to make a difference. He wants others to know what he has come to love. He seems to have discovered for himself a similarity in the kind of devotion required and in the experience of holistic understanding of our place in nature that is most loosely defined as a religious experience.

After 4 hours sitting in his kitchen, I confessed the real reason why I had come to see him. I had heard the story of Rory coaching and coaxing a novice through the Marathon des Sables. To run the Spartathlon I was going to need his help. He looked at me from head to toe. 'You need to lose 10 kilos in eleven months. Do everything I tell you and you might have a chance.'

We agreed that I would return to Derby later that month and he would start me on a training regime.

'And you should come to Rotherham.'

'Rotherham?'

'Fifty miles through the mud. You'll love it.'

Bed for the night was a sleeping bag in a sports hall outside Doncaster, a privilege for which I paid £4. There was to be no great pasta feast or grand ceremony the night before the race as on the marathon circuit. There was a Tesco's around the corner, but those of us who arrived early ate tinned spaghetti carbonara at a local pub.

The 50 miles could be run or walked, with the walkers rising first at 4 a.m. I tried to ignore them and get a last shot of sleep, but now that we were only hours away from starting I just wanted to get on with it. Around me some of the elite runners were already drinking tea and eating Weetabix warmed up over campfire stoves. Unshaven and unhurried, they were dressed in shorts and flimsy raincoats, torn at the elbow, which would not keep the rain out for long. They ate in silence, exchanging smiles and nods with those they knew as we listened to the wind trying to tear off the corrugated iron roof from corner to corner. It had already been raining for twelve hours and the forecast was getting worse. It was even rumoured that the farmers had ploughed the fields 'especially for us'. The sound of the scourging wind and lashing rain was a thrillingly belittling experience, and I could not wait to get started.

Taking off my T-shirt to change into my running kit revealed the curvature of my stomach muscles, which I had been working at for two months and which was the source of quiet, unspoken pride. All the work I had put in immediately became meaningless next to the sinewy, tattooed bodies around me. Striding across the hall came a runner in his sixties, his legs like those of a horse, the coarse fibre that held muscle to bone flexing with every step. His body reminded me of the sculptor Anthony Gormley's installation on the beach at Crosby, where hundreds of identical statues had once stood with their backs to the shore, gazing out towards the horizon. He said of his sculpture, as he could have said of these men and women, that they were the image of 'no hero, no ideal, just the industrially reproduced body of a middle-aged man trying to remain standing and trying to breathe'. Even having run seven marathons, I was some way out of my depth. You don't wake up one morning and decide to become an ultra-distance runner; you take your body to the sea and let the elements beat the privilege into you. Compared to these runners I was a leaking old hulk, swarming with rats and covered in barnacles.

I was part of a group of eight, all friends of Rory's and veterans of numerous ultras. Diggers had broken his ankle on this race two years earlier and had still finished. Killers was preparing for an ultra-triathlon race, consisting of a run from Marble Arch in London to Dover, a cross-Channel swim and then a cycle ride to the Arc de Triomphe in Paris. The weather today treated us all with equal contempt and, with 5 minutes to go, as we made our final preparations, the foghorn sounded. Head torches gave off a sodium haze in the winter rain, as we shuffled towards the start line. In 12 hours' time we would be back in the rain and the dark, but, like Tennyson's Light Brigade, not the 600.

The loneliness of the long-distance runner is a state

that long ago entered the non-runner's lexicon to explain an intangible impulse. Being alone for hours with no distractions, and with oxygen-rich blood pumping around the body and the brain, is the opportunity for what ultra-distance runner Mark Cockbain calls a 'deep-clean' of the soul. Uncontrolled, it can lead to a kind of madness with disconnected words, fragmented sentences or repeated phrases circulating endlessly in a nonsensical, internalised dialogue. I had been nervous that, in a dark moment, when the idea of quitting tempted me, I would capitulate just to get the voices out of my head. But from the moment that Rory reined us in so that we went off last, the chatter was ceaseless. For them it was just another day out with friends. They were as excited as schoolchildren let out into the country air.

No ultra-distance marathon in the UK can be run continuously since such races are predominantly plotted through the fields, fells or hills of the Midlands, Scotland or along the Jurassic coast. But ultra-walking is not a Blakean stroll down country lanes. There is no place for the rustic walker with a crooked stick in one hand and an ear of wheat clamped between the teeth, nor is there time to lament the dark satanic, and now defunct, mills of Sheffield's outer perimeter. Bent at the elbow, the arms need to stiffen as the body's weight is shifted onto the balls of the feet to generate forward propulsion. With every incline the call would go up from

Rory, 'And we're walking.' We crashed into each other on the first hill, not expecting the order to come up so soon, but quickly got the hang of it.

My teeth began to chatter uncontrollably almost the moment we left behind the hot drinks and damp warmth of the cricket pavilion at the halfway checkpoint with 6 hours on the clock. Seated by the steamed-up window, those who had given up blew on their tea as we changed into dry kit. The skin on my feet had become blanched and wrinkled, loosened from the flesh beneath. I was told that it would get easier.

The fields were as grey and bleak as the sea, the familiar, toneless colour of metal. Geese cronked overhead. For the next 5 miles the earth held firm as we stumbled on. Even so, by the afternoon I was in difficulty. For some time we moved across fields with no shadow of a path. Climbing fences and pushing through hedges was beginning to so exhaust and annoy me that, when I finally emerged from a huge ploughed field at 35 miles, I was ready to cry with rage. I started to swear out loud and snarl, real tears pricking my eyes. I rested for a moment against a gate. On Sunday-morning training runs I had quit for less than this. Rory sensed my hesitation. 'It's too late to turn back. You're staying with us.'

The light was already starting to dwindle as we passed through the ruins of an abbey and into the woods towards the final checkpoint. The landscape around me was growing richer; but it was a winter richness of scrubbed to dull silver, glowering rain-washed bricks and hedges picked as clean as skeletons. As night rapidly fell once more, all the sounds of day faded as the most desperate of creatures, having braved the elements, returned to hibernation. Halfway through the forest, like a bird's song cut off mid-verse, the group suddenly fell silent as we slowed to a walk for the 20-minute incline. With our head torches not yet back on, the loss of sound and light became total.

In the silence we dropped Ben from the group as he slowed to a walk. He was also a marathon runner, but had never done anything like this before either. We tried to cajole him with fruit pastilles and the promise of jam sandwiches at the next checkpoint, but he shook his head. He looked as if he would have sat down and given up altogether if we had protested too much, so we had no choice but to leave him.

The half-hour spent skirting Sheffield, passing under the M1 and wading through the plastic bags and detritus of millions of commuters, was the closest we came to seeing anyone all day. There were football matches to come home from and dinners to prepare. Drivers, oblivious to their surroundings and keen to get home as quickly as possible, choked us with their exhaust fumes. Following the nauseating, sucking sound of feet squelching through mud took all my effort. Far up ahead, coming over the crest of a hill whose breach could not be ascertained in this pitiful Midlands darkness, were the torchlights of another team, staggering drunkenly as if atop the mast of a ship at sea, and I recalled poems of the First World War memorised at school.

Bent double, like old beggars under sacks,
Knock-kneed, coughing like hags, we cursed through
     sludge,
Till on the haunting flares we turned our backs
And towards our distant rest began to trudge.

The 40-minute lessons, which our humourless teacher spent hammering in the virtues of Wilfred Owen's 'Dulce et Decorum Est', were devoid of either joy or comprehension, but it was my own lack of imagination that completely failed to link these poems to the events taught in double history down the corridor on Tuesday mornings. None of this occurred to me as I ploughed through the thick soil and heavy air as we lurched home. It was only months later, when the flash of Rory's head torch came into my memory, that I thought back to the classroom and connected the oozing mud, which had made my legs so heavy that it would have been easier to capitulate than go on, with the landscape and images that Owen had captured on the page.

The novelist Haruki Murakami wrote of his first ultra-marathon: 'at the end I hardly knew who I was, or what I was doing. This should have been a very alarming feeling, but it didn't feel that way. By then running had entered the realm of the metaphysical.' I felt none of this. Twelve hours after we had started, we turned back into the industrial estate and were into the final mile. As we ran alongside the filth of a stagnant canal, a momentary shimmer on the surface suggested a bloated body floating beneath the surface. Rory suddenly speeded up. We had already covered 49 miles and yet he made it a sprint finish. I tried to keep up, but could find no more momentum, and I crept slowly towards the finish line.

In the safety of the sports hall I devoured the shepherd's pie made by the volunteers, the real heroes of this adventure, who had spent the whole day watching out for us. Then I peeled off layers and had a cold shower before being carried by Rory one last time to the train station for home. With my rucksack at my feet, I sat back to let exhaustion take hold of me for the duration of the journey. I started sweating almost immediately and shaking profusely, my teeth clattering together uncontrollably in my head, my limbs going into spasm as though from an electric shock. I was overcome by a hypoglycaemic fit as my blood sugar levels dropped. As I scrabbled with the zips of my rucksack to find a bar of chocolate, the train jerked to a halt at Doncaster station. I fell to the floor, spilling the contents of my bag. Two girls, who had sat opposite me on their way into town for a night out, stood up. I started to motion that I was fine and did not need their help, but they had already stepped over my legs and were laughing at me from the platform edge as the doors closed behind them. I shoved the chocolate in my mouth, before climbing to my knees, hauling myself onto the seat and falling asleep.

For days afterwards I would wake in fright hours before dawn, my limbs paralysed. Even turning my ankle against the weight of the duvet was an insurmountable challenge, to roll on my side an impossibility.

The history of ultra-distance running competitions is an inexact one. While both Wordsworth and Dickens wrote of watching guides race across the fells of Cumbria, and footnotes exist of these long-distance races from around 1064, until the mid nineteenth century few people had room in their lives for formalised rituals of competitive exertion. As E. P. Thompson, the author of *The Making of the Working Class*, might have written, the rich were too busy hunting and fighting to worry about long-distance races, and the poor were too busy surviving and being oppressed. Samuel Pepys's diaries from 1663, however, do tell of races in which servants were pitted against one another, constrained only by the speed of their masters' carriages. During this time, fell-running flourished, but had only a functional role – to gain employment as a guide rather than competing for prize money – and it was not until the arrival of the Victorians, who always itched for a challenge, that running for a wager became a popular pastime. In 1864 pedestrianism was introduced to the annual Oxford and Cambridge athletics meetings, the first formalisation of competitive athletics.

In a sport that has long ceased to be fashionable, Robert Barclay Allardice was, and still is, the most famous pedestrian to have ever lived. He was born in Scotland in 1777 into a family who spent their spare time wrestling bulls and uprooting trees barehanded. Although his family was eccentric – he was a keen bare-knuckle boxer as well – these were not unique feats, at a time when tests of endurance were enjoyed as spectacles of mass entertainment. However, it was his extraordinary walking feats that earned Barclay his greatest renown and the title of the 'Celebrated Pedestrian'.

By the eighteenth century the events recorded by Pepys had morphed into long-distance walking events that attracted huge crowds. It could also be extremely lucrative for its top competitors, particularly if, like Barclay, they were not averse to a degree of gamesmanship to stack up the odds. In 1801, he wagered 1,000 guineas that he could walk 90 miles in 21 hours, but caught a cold and lost. He then increased the stake to 2,000 guineas and lost again. He then got odds that would pay him 5,000 guineas if he won, which he did, with an hour to spare.

Tens of miles soon became hundreds, as road races

were brought indoors for people to watch and bet enormous amounts of money on. By 1878, pedestrianism had become so popular as a spectator and gambling sport that Sir John Astley MP founded a 'Long-Distance Championship of the World'. Organised over six days, it was inspired by a desire to clean up the perception that pedestrianism was corrupted by gambling, as well as to codify it as an amateur sport. In 1908 it was included in the Olympic Games.

The Golden Age of pedestrianism had arrived. Because of the wobbly gait of some of the competitors, the format was altered to allow people to walk or run at any time, as they competed for the Astley Belt, which was made out of solid silver and gold and valued at a staggering £100. A purse of £500 was the real prize, though, with the winner of three races in a row being declared the permanent victor. By the time pedestrianism took centre stage in America, at the end of the nineteenth century, winners could expect to pick up $50,000 after just two races. In 1867, Edward Payson Weston, a reporter for the *New York Herald*, won a $10,000 prize by walking 1,136 miles from Portland, Maine, to Chicago in thirty days. In a peculiar take on the sport, in 1871, he then walked 200 miles backwards around St Louis.

Barclay's most impressive feat was to walk 1 mile every hour for 1,000 hours, which Walter Thom documented in his book of 1813, *Pedestrianism*. His 'astonishing exploits', which nearly killed him, were achieved between 1 June and 12 July 1809, when he set off in a top hat, woollen suit and cravat, carrying a silver-topped walking stick. Barclay added a chapter of his own, describing his training methods that put his success down to a diet of stout beer and milk consumed before naps taken 'naked on clean white sheets', a regime that was quickly adopted by those who attempted to emulate the feat.

In 2003, David Bedford re-created Barclay's 1,000-mile challenge, asking Rory to join a team that would complete the 1,000 miles and finish by running the full distance of the London Marathon. Rather than collapsing at the end into woozy hysteria, the team achieved their goal easily. Against expectations, when they came to run the marathon they struggled because they had lost fitness, rather than because of exhaustion – testament to the improved diets and exercise regimes that are now part of the runner's daily routine.

Although there were famous instances of competitors taking to the countryside – most notably in the Great American Race that ran from the east to the west coast – to benefit the crowds of spectators, most races took place indoors on a track of roughly 400 metres. The most spectacular exception was Mensen Ernst, a Norwegian seaman, born in 1795. Known in the navy to be a brilliant runner, he made a living by placing bets on himself to run certain distances within a set time, starting with a 116-kilometre race from London to Portsmouth, which he did in 9 hours. This, however, was nothing compared to the epic runs that he would later achieve as he ran from continent to continent. In 1832, he followed the route taken by Napoleon in his march on Moscow two decades earlier. The sum of 100,000 francs had been bet by the time he left and Ernst was to receive 3,800 francs if he covered the distance in fifteen days. Leaving from Place Vendôme in Paris, he ran the 1,760 miles to Moscow in thirteen days and 18 hours, averaging over 120 miles a day.

'I felt I was sailing . . . on my two unique frigates,' he was quoted as saying later. 'Those who witnessed my running considered me eccentric, or else a fool, or possessed by the devil.' The *New York Times* called it a 'wonderful and incredible performance'. The stunt made him a hero and he spent the following years taking his one-man circus from city to city, re-enacting his adventures for royal audiences. In 1836, the East India Company paid him £250 to run from Constantinople to Calcutta as a publicity stunt, which he did in four weeks. After a three-day rest, he ran back again – 8,900 kilometres in fifty-nine days.

According to a contemporary German biographer, Ernst's motto was 'Motion is life, stagnation is death.' Although he carried a map with him, along with a sextant and all his provisions, he would always plot the most direct route, never skirting around a mountain when he could run over it, never taking a detour downstream to find a bridge when he could swim across. In the spring of 1842, thirty years before Stanley and Livingstone had their historic encounter in Africa, the German author, proprietor and adventurer, Count Hermann von Pückler-Muskau, asked Mensen to find the source of the White Nile. He ran from Muskau in Prussia down through the Ottoman Empire to Jerusalem in thirty days and then ran the 500 kilometres to Cairo. Although he had faced almost every extreme that the elements could offer, one morning he was found by locals under a tree, a handkerchief covering his face. He had died from dysentery, most likely carried in the water he drank. His remains now rest next to the Aswan Dam. A Norwegian newspaper declared: 'The world will never see his like again.'

There are few clues to his success. Whereas Barclay ate and drank like a lion, Ernst survived the extreme conditions across Russia, and later Asia and the subcontinent, on a strict diet of bread, cheese and a few vegetables, avoiding hot food altogether. He fidgeted terribly, never sleeping for more than a few hours at a time, and when he did sleep it was always outdoors, since he believed that lying on hard ground kept his body supple. His only weakness was for wine, which he used to consume by the bottle, even as he ran.

★

Rory had insisted that I needed to do at least two sessions a week in the gym, whose membership I had retained but had rarely used in any of my training for previous marathons. To improve my VO_2 max capacity, he put me on a programme of weights and running that would strain every sinew as it sent the blood flow first to my head and then to my feet. My brain, though, was buzzing with the adventures I would encounter out running, and I was reluctant, at first, to get caught up in the claustrophobia of exercising indoors.

The emphasis in modern gyms, as opposed to their Greek or Victorian predecessors, is on comfort and luxury. Members are supplied with limitless, soft, warm towels, handcream and hair gel, and are confronted at every turn by floor-to-ceiling mirrors to gratify their vanity. Even as recently as the Victorian period, the purpose of such places was to provide certain tools that crafted the athlete and were considered necessary to prepare him for the open road.

By contrast, the modern gym claims to offer 'an holistic experience' that will 'harmonise' our physical and mental well-being. Gyms are packed with exercise classes that create a wholesale replacement of our athletic experience of nature by asking us to imagine our way out of dimly lit rooms into the wilds of the mountains. The twenty-first-century athlete is a busy person, always short of time. Every compartment of our lives is catered for by technology, which allows us to meet our least requirement more efficiently. The role of the gym today is to provide a package in which an athletic experience can be condensed into a 45-minute session so that afterwards we can get on with the rest of our day as swiftly as possible. Given this dominant perception of what modern athleticism should feel like – that is, running through landscapes – ignoring signposts and one-way systems seems positively subversive.

While to be cut off from nature went against everything that running stood for, to be forced into the gym did clarify my sense of why I ran at all. It showed me that running was about adventure, exploration, subversion – all the things the gym could never deliver. Each time I went, it made the next run that much more pleasurable. Through gritted teeth I clanked the hulking frames of the weights machines in an air-conditioned hall filled with treadmills, the only satisfaction coming when I left one evening, having leg-pressed a quarter of a ton of cold steel in an empty room.

On the now-ubiquitous treadmill, the very purpose of motion is reduced to a single, immovable point. The physical sensation of space itself, as with landscape, has been reduced to the dimension of a television screen. James Gleick despaired of the eternal horizon of the treadmill: 'you must be aware that this march is almost by definition a waste of time, made possible by the luxury of time, made necessary by the disappearance of backbreaking labour from the daily routine.' It is a sterilised experience that is highly disorientating, eventually leading to a complete divorce between natural athletic expression and the open road. For the runners on the treadmill, with the day's news pouring from the wall of plasma screens, all athletic expression has been neutered. At the push of a button we can bring the finish line to us the moment we stray out of our comfort zone. As Rebecca Solnit writes: 'The treadmill . . . accommodates the mind which is more comfortable with quantifiable and clearly defined activity than with the seamless engagement of the mind, body and terrain to be found outdoors.' In other words, the modern gym caters for the sentimental athlete who wants to have the luxury of the experience of athletic exertion without having to pay the physical or mental price for it. For twelve months I went for 2 hours twice a week without fail, and I hated every minute of it.

To learn what the ingredients were to becoming an ultra-distance runner, it was not enough to simply push back the limits of my physical capacity. There was a profound psychological leap that I needed to make, which could not be done just by running, but required learning from other sporting arenas. In a century of high speed and instantaneousness, we would do well to learn from those who walked before us. One such was Rousseau, for whom the solitude of the experience brought together the mind and body, to a point where thinking became almost a physical, rhythmical act. As he wrote, 'When I stop, I cease to think; my mind only works with my legs.'

The dreaming mind is usually bodiless and generates a peculiar power in locomotion. Sometimes, as I ran in the dark, I would turn off the head torch and force myself to run faster and faster over the uneven surface. Leaving behind the city lights, my body, as a physical object, disappeared. With my arms swinging, launching myself into the darkness was the closest I have ever come to weightlessness. It was only when the street lighting returned to me the silhouette of my physical body that I came back to earth. Very briefly running in complete darkness, away from the hollow din of other people, can lead to a kind of ecstasy.

It is not just the runner who can conjure up this weightless abandonment. For the swimmer, the water can become a dream world too as the waves close behind her, concealing her watery path as she becomes fully submerged. I have always been drawn to water and the 'intensely sensuous involvement, a rhythmic succession of sounds as the hands cut through the water' of swimming, as Murray Rose called it. In Charles Sprawson's intoxicating cultural history of swimming, he identifies the principal quality demanded of the swimmer as a 'feel for water', which attracts those 'remote and divorced from everyday life, devoted to a mode of exercise where most of the body remains submerged and self-absorbed'. The physiologically divine Johnny Weissmuller, double

Olympic swimming gold-medallist and the original Tarzan, understood well the importance of sensitivity in the search for the most ergonomic path through the water. Swimming does not equal muscle power. Instead it is bound to efficiency, natural rhythm and the path of least resistance.

The search for this feeling, too, can lead to an obsessive madness, since much of the swimmer's training takes place inside her head and the long hours spent semi-submerged can induce a lonely, meditative state of mind. Immersed as she is in a continuous dream of a world under water, so intense and concentrated are her conditions that the swimmer becomes prey to delusions and neuroses beyond the experience of other athletes. For Sprawson, it is precisely this locked-in sensation that draws many people to the water. 'Like Narcissus, many of the swimmers suffered from a form of autism, a self-encapsulation in an isolated world.' In this way, what connected swimmers like Byron and Swinburne was that they were 'generally out of harmony with their age, idealists who felt deeply the futility of life, the contrast between what life is and what it ought to be. It was as though water, like opium, provided the swimmers with a heightened existence, a refuge from the everyday life they loathed.'

Like the runner, the swimmer too can lay claim to a subversive nature, one that revolts against society's conventions and finds its first expression in Goethe and German

Romanticism. Goethe drew a dividing line between those who pined for a return to the old pastoral and pagan world that delighted in the naked body and in water, and the obedient flocks who still adhered to the precepts of medieval morality. Like Coubertin, Goethe sentimentalised the Ancient Greeks and their way of life. Given the cultural attitudes that had followed in their wake, Goethe saw the Ancients as people who lived 'in accordance with nature, free from constraints', unlike Goethe himself. While Coubertin took from the Greeks the notion of structure, moral duty and relentless self-improvement, Goethe realised that swimming, as the Greeks had swum, offered the possibility of eternal freedom.

This expression of freedom was first captured visually by Leni Riefenstahl, in *Olympia*, arguably one of the greatest sports films ever produced. After the huge success of her Nazi epic, *Triumph of the Will*, she was commissioned by the International Olympic Committee, with the enthusiastic backing of Hitler, to cover the spectacle of the 1936 Berlin Olympics. It also happened to be an effective propaganda tool. For Hitler, the 220-minute film was designed as a paean to Aryan superiority, making a direct link between the strong-limbed German athletes and the gods of the ancient Olympic Games. Nevertheless, no film, before or since, has so convincingly portrayed the aesthetics of the athlete in motion.

Riefenstahl wanted to shoot a comprehensive documentation of the Games that was devoted to the body in motion. As a former dancer, she was drawn to the sensual qualities of grace and movement, and wanted to replicate this on the track and field. 'You only see the beauty,' she exulted. The result is a film suffused with eroticism. In order to demonstrate the godlike features of the athletes, she built a human bridge between classical Greece and the New Germany. 'I could see the ancient ruins of the classical Olympic sites slowly emerging from patches of fog and the Greek temples and sculptures drifting by,' she explained. 'That was my vision for the prologue of my *Olympia*.' This is precisely how the film opens, although the sculptures dissolve to living nudes. She even appears here herself, uncredited, as a nude dancer.

She filmed 'everything' of the Berlin Games from 'every conceivable angle', by mounting cameras beneath balloons, on rafts, in trenches and under saddles, to try to capture the effort of performance. For the marathon sequence, tiny cameras were attached to the runners' necks to film their feet pounding the paved course, showing the ordeal from as subjective a viewpoint as possible, whilst delivering her preconceived notion of the athelete's struggle – metronomic, radiant and heroic. Long shots across wheat fields made the explicit connection between the runners and our natural state as creatures of motion. The music builds to an orgasmic crescendo as the trumpets sound to signal the runners' entry into the stadium for the final lap. The tempo of both music and runners then dwindles as if slipping into a post-coital slumber. In the editing she slowed down the footage to convey the onset of exhaustion. As she explained in her first-person perspective of the event, 'I am the marathon!'

It was said of the dancer Nijinsky that when he leapt he seemed to stop in midair. Riefenstahl's own past informed her understanding of the grace of the human physique as she filmed *Olympia*. But it is with the diving competition, the climax of the film, that *Olympia* is at its visually most ravishing.

Filming from under the water, she could follow the divers in a single shot, as they first swooped out of the clouds from the board into the pool, then burst to the surface in a jewel-like constellation of bubbles. For these sequences she seemed to have been less and less concerned with recording the events than with the divers performing their acts. As the shots are cut to confuse the direction from which the diver is coming, the law of gravity itself seems to be suspended as the diver enjoys the complete freedom of weightlessness before hitting the water. His body arches like that of Icarus, falling and surfacing again. These shots convey an almost religious devotion to the grace of the human form and the power of liberation through movement. This is what Rory had meant when he talked about the privilege of the running experience.

★

Races that I entered as I worked towards the crescendo of the Spartathlon took me 40 miles up the Grand Union canal, 30 miles over the South Downs, across the self-proclaimed 'Toughest Marathon in Britain', and with Alex, who I had run with at school, around the course of the London Marathon, but in reverse, from the finishing post to the start line at 4 a.m. on the day of the race. There was also the 100-kilometre race around the forests of Amsterdam, which I succeeded in completing in less than the 10 hours 30 minutes required to qualify for the Spartathlon. Improbable as it seems, I came fourth, beaten only by a Dutch runner who had come third in the Spartathlon ten years earlier and two veterans of the ultra-distance circuit.

These races were tough but went uncelebrated since they were merely stepping stones towards a single goal. To describe what it felt like to run them would be to misrepresent their significance, since I told almost no one about them and ran them all, except for the forty-four laps around the forest in Amsterdam, after a 100-mile week. I reported back to Rory matter-of-factly on my progress, and went out of my way to run alone in order to try to replicate the pressure and exhaustion that I anticipated feeling in Greece. Exhausting as these races were, I could not yet begin to imagine what it would feel like to be on my feet for 36 hours non-stop.

While nothing much changed on the surface – although by the time I got to Athens I had lost 10 kilos

– beneath the skin I underwent a very subtle psychological shift. Over a period of months it became clear
to me that a marathon is not that great a distance for
those of us who will never trouble the winners. So long
as we keep below the lactic acid radar – the point at
which the body starts to poison itself through the pollution of the bloodstream – then our muscles can recover
quickly, restoring the kinetic energy deep within that
keeps one foot stepping out in front of the other.

While the miles I covered were mostly about strengthening and expanding my muscles to cope with the long
hours that I would spend on my feet, for the first time
I was also learning that the view of the true runner is
like that of a sailor on the ocean. He pierces the horizon
and watches the point at which he did so recede in his
wake. The world that I wanted to inhabit was one that
poured away on either side of me: a universe of no
attachments, of disappearing plains. An existence of pure
motion. I wanted to be like the best ultra-distance
runners who skimmed and floated an inch above the
ground, small and buoyant, drifting on the air like a
sycamore seed.

I came to see that those who had not taught themselves to run were anchored to the ground, earthbound,
lumbered with a perspective that was without patterns
or sequences stuck in one dimension. When you start
to see this, then the true magnificence of long-distance
running is revealed. One January, Fred Lebow, the creator

of the New York City Marathon, planned to run 2,500 miles in a year. His girlfriend left him when he cancelled a dinner invitation to get in another 19 miles before the year was out, only to discover that he had long since exceeded his target. As flat-headed as he was to not know when to stop, what his girlfriend did not understand was that it was not about the miles as such; it was about the world that is revealed in motion, one that she could not see.

As the date of the Spartathlon came closer, I saw that the possibility of success hinged on the smallest considerations and the size of the sacrifice that I was prepared to make. To run twice a day every day and put in the long miles at the weekend meant forgoing friendships, family and the mundane pleasures of everyday life.

In physiological terms I was teaching myself to hold off the moment at which the system ceases to be able to convert glucose and carbohydrates into energy and starts to consume itself. There is a limit to all physical capacity, a point at which the body can do no more, but the runner must learn to live right at the edge between the superhuman and flesh-and-blood vulnerability. It is no coincidence that, at two Olympic Games, Paula Radcliffe succumbed to the kind of stomach bug and stress fracture that would be almost unheard of in sedentary life. Her level of fitness, with so little fat on her body, put her at a level of risk that most of us will never face.

These signs of mortality, where a miscalculated run would end in bleeding or vomiting, were some of the only totems of improvement that I brought home. It was not until two months before the Spartathlon that I found, quite literally, that muscles I had never seen before had appeared down my thighs and calves. A photograph taken on the last decline at the Picnic Marathon in June caught the moment my foot struck the ground. The ricochet of the impact up the leg revealed not flesh and bone, but knotted steel.

The one-line email from Iain came through on a list-less May afternoon. 'Do you fancy having a go at the Bob Graham Round?'

I was now into the last three months of training and was running two full marathons at the weekend during my 120-mile week. To keep pushing back the boundaries of fatigue, I scheduled an ultra-marathon every three weeks from the beginning of July to the middle of September. Inevitably I came across familiar faces and we would greet each other with nods of appreciation as we lined up to start. We did not need to explain to one another why we were here. On days when it was too hot to sit still for long, there was nothing else that we would rather be doing other than running 30 miles across the South Downs.

Iain and I had never run together. He had recently cycled solo from Land's End to John O'Groats, and was a much more experienced ultra-runner, having completed the Marathon des Sables and finished the Round Rotherham 2 full hours faster than I had. I could not possibly refuse such an offer.

Since Bob Graham first set off over forty-two peaks of the Lake District, on a course that would eventually take his name, no one has been able to calculate the exact distance of the run. The best guess is 72 miles, which is some way from the '140 miles' over '30,000 feet of climbing' that it was estimated he had covered in 1932 when he succeeded, on his second attempt, in making the round. It is a race that takes most runners four attempts, and I was under no illusion: we were likely to fail. The most attractive challenge for my schedule was the chance to practise being on my feet for the 24 hours allowed to finish the round. I was not surprised at how quickly I accepted.

The first recorded round of the fells was made by a clergyman from Cambridge, J. M. Elliott, in 1864, when he covered Scafell Pike and eight other peaks in 8½ hours. In 1904, it was a local doctor who wrote that his own aim was 'to ascend the greatest possible number of peaks over 2,000 feet, and return to the starting point within twenty-four hours'. These became the basic rules of the challenge.

By the time Bob Graham made his attempt, the challenge had developed from fell-walking to fell-running. At 1 a.m. in the middle of June 1932 he set off from the clock tower of Moot Hall in Keswick, first towards Threlkeld and then to Clough Head. His only training had been long walks over the fells during the night. Wearing plimsolls, shorts and his pyjama top, he completed the round, like Ernst, sustained on rations of bread and butter and lightly boiled eggs. He set a record that stood for twenty-eight years, although each year numerous attempts were made to beat it.

Over the decades the challenge morphed from speed to distance, climaxing with Joss Naylor covering each of the 214 summits named by fell writer Alfred Wainwright – 391 miles and over 121,000 feet of ascent – in seven days, 1 hour and 25 minutes. For us, though, trained on a diet of London's pavements, forty-two peaks was quite enough.

On the way up on the first day of summer through the holiday traffic, we talked in detail about what sandwiches we would like at the various checkpoints, changes of clothes and the weather, barely exchanging a word on what the run itself would require from us. We planned to start at midnight, aware that the sun was due to rise around 3.30 a.m. After a meal at a Little Chef, we tried to get a few hours' sleep at the adjacent Travel Lodge in the last hours of daylight. Arriving in Keswick, we watched a ball of light barrelling down Clough Head, a comet brought down to earth by gravity. If we were on schedule, we would be ascending that slope, whose contours were hidden from us in the dark, in less than 5 hours' time.

Over Skiddaw there moved a purple-blue light in shooting pyramids. It never quite got dark and the mountains were menacing, low, huddled together. There was not a murmur of sound from traffic, running water or even wind, and the full moon had risen over the mountains to a perfect altitude. Our extended fingers ascended effortlessly over the darkness. We pointed towards our first peak and waited for midnight to strike.

By 1.22 a.m. we were on the roof of the Lake District, just in touch with a group that had set off before us, as we avoided a two-man tent pitched at the summit. From Skiddaw we went into our first descent. Bob Graham had said that he enjoyed the ascents because it was a chance to rest. Watching the lights ahead slip into the darkness as we tentatively jogged down the hill, taking care not to twist an ankle, we understood what he meant. Twenty minutes later, at the next checkpoint, the other group had put 5 minutes between us. It was on these descents that we were supposed to make up all the lost time, but we were not used to having to pick our way through heather and rocks. A haze of mist appeared in the beam of our head torches as our breath condensed, clouding our vision of where we might step next. With no path to follow, we trailed the footprints in the dew of those who had preceded us.

We lost the leading torches again into the rich, Indian-ink darkness of the valley untouched by the moonlight, and although we had been moving for only 3 hours it was clear that we were already starting to lose time. Rocks, mounds and entire peaks were indistinguishable, open to misinterpretation, and in the dark we completely lost all perspective. A small cairn that we were supposed to turn right at, and were pleased to have found so easily in the dark, was in fact the full face of the peak half a mile away that we had to ascend. Down we went again in the heather, waist deep, through patches of tall grass shimmering in the faintest of light, and the contrast created the illusion that we were running towards floods of water. With Iain behind me, I picked my way through as best I could until I stepped right into a hidden stream, which consumed legs, body and light. At 3.26 a.m. we had made the third of the forty-two ascents and below us, for the first time, were dotted the lights of the village of Threlkeld.

I took a step forward and saw how we had to get off the mountain. Although there was not enough light yet to reveal any kind of path, it seemed to me that we would have to run along the edge of a knife to get down off the mountain, each side of it falling away over a wild, savage precipice into valleys whose finality could not yet be seen. The headlights of the leading group had almost disappeared now. The magic of the grand outlines in front of us, and the perpetual shapes that denoted our course, held me in an almost religious grip. This was intensified no doubt by the primitiveness of my experience of them, since I lived in a world of flat planes and two-dimensional paths that ran in almost straight lines from A to B. Samuel Coleridge, much of whose Romantic poetry had been inspired by these hills, had responded in his notebook in a similar way: 'a thick palpable Blue up to the moon/save that at the very top of the blue the clouds rolled lead-coloured – small detachments of these clouds running in thick flakes near the moon, & drinking its light in amber & white. – The moon in a clear azure sky – the Mountains seen indeed, and only seen – I never saw aught so sublime!'

While the notion of the sublime has long been a part of our vocabulary, it was not until Edmund Burke addressed the idea, using an empirical method based on his own psychological experience, that the sublime came out of the lecture hall and into the living room. Burke's *A Philosophical Enquiry into the Origins of Our Ideas of the Sublime and Beautiful* is obsessed by bodily representation of the experience of the sublime and the responses of the human mind to its emotive manifestations. His theory addresses the power and the immediacy of this evocation. For Burke the sublime could inspire a delightful horror. 'Whatever is fitted in any sort to excite the ideas of pain, and danger, that is to say, whatever is in any sort terrible . . . is a source of the sublime; that is, it is productive of the strongest emotion which the mind is capable of feeling.' But it must not come too close. 'When danger or pain press too nearly, they are incapable of giving any delight, and are simply terrible;

but at certain distances, and with certain modifications, they may be, and they are delightful.' The sublime in nature appears as a form of paralysis. We have no control over it, are transfixed by our confrontation with it, and are reduced to a state of submission that disorientates and dominates.

But while he wrote from the comfort of his study that 'whatever is qualified to cause terror, is a foundation capable of the sublime', Burke's interpretation is really a kind of behind-the-sofa mock horror, since we can enjoy it only from a position of safety. 'Whatever is fitted to produce such a tension [as terror], must be productive of a passion similar to terror, and consequently must be a source of the sublime, though it should have no idea of danger connected with it.'

Days and weeks later, when I reflected on stepping out onto that knife edge, I could no longer gauge whether I had been truly afraid or not.

'Would you like me to lead?' Iain had asked.

'If you wouldn't mind.'

All the radiance of that experience was diluted once it was over. From the safety of my living room, when I recounted our adventure the fear became an abstraction, an experience known only in the third person. 'Self-discovery comes when a man measures himself against an obstacle,' wrote the French aviation pioneer, Antoine de Saint-Exupéry. When that obstacle is an object of sublime horror, it turns our faculties inside out and all we can do is to submit ourselves to it, to throw ourselves at its feet. It is at this point of vertigo, or in the pleasure of verticality, that the fell-runner and the road-runner diverge. One confronts an authentic, tangible danger; the other is generating an obstacle in the form of the pain of running further and further. And in that danger we try to give landscape meaning, character, to call it sublime – anything to get some purchase on it, no matter how fleeting, to help us get down safely.

It is not surprising that Coleridge dismissed Burke's psychological assessment of the sublime. In his turn, he said that 'My philosophical opinions are blended with or deduced from my feelings', and that 'if impressions and ideas constitute our Being, [then] I shall have a tendency to become a God – so sublime & beautiful will be the series of my visual existence'. His *Notebooks* covering his 'Walking Tours' of 1802 tell of a spatial history of topographical engagement as well as of the reflections of a man who took to the Lakes to turn himself inside out and see what he could find.

From Keswick, between 1 and 9 August 1802, he set off on a nine-day physical and imaginative journey in search of perfect solitude, in a deliberate and self-conscious act of liberation from the suffocation of family life. He called it a circumcursion – a delimiting of spatial experience. He wanted to have his claustrophobia surrounded, and he recorded a series of *plein air* sketches that not only capture the physical sensation of the runner

– 'as I bounded down, I noticed the moving stones under the soft moss, hurting my feet' – but also the spiritual effect of moving alone through such a vast, wild and desolate landscape.

What Coleridge provided as a route to his solitude was a detailed articulation of the embodied experience of the geography and geology of the Cumbrian terrain. The mountains came up through his boots leaving his feet lusciously bruised and he was no longer perceiving them from afar. 'To *think* of a thing is different from to *perceive it*, as "to walk" is from "to feel the ground under you".' It was a new form of Romantic writing – rapid, instantaneous. Coleridge's biographer, Richard Holmes, calls it 'like a music score', and Coleridge lamented those who came to the Lakes 'passing by the very places instead of looking at the places'. Anyone who has scaled Scafell Pike or Helvellyn will know that the fells often bring moments of intense vision, and the urge to climb out of civilisation, of ourselves even, to get above and beyond the stale crust of daily life. It was these very places that formed the basis of his comprehension of his surroundings. 'We understand Nature just as if at a distance we looked at the Image of a Person in a Looking-glass, plainly and fervently discoursing – yet what he uttered, we could decypher only by the motion of the Lips, and the mien, and the expression of the muscles of the Countenance.' Stranded at the summit of Scafell on 2 August 1802, with no immediate way down as a storm raged around him, he was overcome by breathlessness and dizziness, racked by a fear that put his 'whole Limbs in a *Tremble*'. This intensely real sensation makes Burke's account of the sublime look like a schoolboy classroom experiment.

I crept, slid and skidded down the damp moss. When I stood and looked down into the vertical chasm, the cliffs now rose up 50, then 60, then 100 feet above us. Through the mist beneath us, we could finally see into a basin ablaze. The birds were beginning to sing as the light changed from macabre to tender in the fullness of a summer's morning. A single pillar of smoke from a farm chimney was just distinguishable from the mist, silhouetted against the solid form of the next peak across the valley that we had to ascend.

We had been up on the hills, almost alone, for nearly 10 hours and their mystical stillness was still impenetrable. In part, this was because I did not have the eyes to see with, but language also failed me. Coleridge knew this failure too. While, for him, the poet was a metaphysician who actively engages with nature, who goes out of himself, who hunts down the otherness of being, as transient runners we are always stopped short of complete transcendence. 'It is easy to cloathe Imaginary Beings with our Thoughts & Feelings; but to send ourselves out of ourselves, to *think* ourselves into the Thoughts & Feelings of Beings in circumstances wholly and strangely different from our own: hic labor, hoc opus: and who has achieved it? Perhaps only Shakespeare.'

Over to our left we could trace the fifteen peaks that we had managed to, if not overcome, then come to terms with. And to our right were the twenty-seven peaks remaining. Our humility in the face of these mountains was complete. We quit, not because we were broken or exhausted, but simply because we had trained nowhere near hard enough on this terrain. Those who completed the Bob Graham did so by running the fells at every opportunity. Yes, we were incredibly fit, but we had no stamina for vertical ascents that went on for 40 or 50 minutes at a time. We were just not ready for it. Our feet became tender too quickly from the pummelling descents and we could not keep on our toes enough to make the ascents easier. We got picked up at the checkpoint as a team of three runners overtook us. They had set off 2 hours after us and were practising the same stage over and over again for a full attempt later in the summer. We got back in the car, showered at the hotel and drove back to London against the oncoming holiday traffic.

As incredible an experience as crossing the fells had been, I had learnt that this kind of vertical running was not for me. What drew me to distance running was the flat road, where I could internalise the pain endured in travelling for hours in a straight line. The following day

I ran 30 miles along the Thames, which felt like a down-hill gallop after what we had returned from.

It was all good practice, though, for the Spartathlon. I was learning while notching up the precious miles. Each of these Herculean runs, successful or not, repre-sented a new etching on my personality that would better equip me for what I would be taking on in the Spartathlon. As I returned to work on Monday morning, having covered 60 miles that weekend without anyone noticing, I remembered the star-struck feeling I had had when I finished in Rotherham and realised just how far I had come in those nine months. I could now say that I was an ultra-distance runner.

6

Metamorphosis

By the first anniversary of her husband's death, my mother-in-law Marie-Jo was back in hospital again, suffering from what could be called the violence of incommunicability. Something had happened to her, something over which she had no control, and she had to wait for it to work itself through her system. The house in France had been empty for months and when we stood there amongst the deserted tables and chairs, the dumb sentimentality was surprising and rather magical. Before Jean-Louis's death we had come to visit only every few months and for a moment as we turned the door handle we still felt a fresh excitement in returning, as though none of this had actually happened.

In the year that had passed we had all turned into that most dangerous of creatures – the amateur psychologist – and the longer my mother-in-law's illness evaded a comprehensive explanation from the doctors, the more time we spent trying to equate what she was going through with some primary cause. We spent hours in the house with the doors left open to billow some life into the rooms, going through a process of scientific reductionism as we looked for that one clue or single particle of her character that could explain everything.

The town where she and Jean-Louis had lived had long been slowly suffocating, and in the years before his death they had talked of moving to Bordeaux when he retired, to be in a city surrounded by the hum of other people. Entire generations were now leaving, never to return, and shops were being boarded up as the population shrank. In the very early morning, the river valley filled with a Teutonic mist. After a few days of sitting around not knowing what to do, I could not help returning to the fields that had been his workplace, looking for an explanation of how these events had come to pass. Grief came accompanied only by questions as to whether it could have been otherwise, not by answers. As if I were a small child peering just over the rim of a car window, travelling through a new landscape – incomplete and transient, visible but immediately passed – this entire experience was novel to me. I would return to the house with no greater understanding than when I had left.

Marie-Jo had accepted that it was only through medical intervention that any possible future could be envisaged, although it was not at all clear what kind of life she could expect. The house was too big for her on her own, and yet not big enough to hold the memories of her husband that lurked in every darkened corner. She had returned here earlier in the year and, when we had left her alone, she had quickly felt threatened by the wilderness around her and had retreated to the safety of her bed for days at a time. She was overwhelmed by the idea of any kind of existence that did not include Jean-Louis. As she struggled to cope, the branches of the trees they had planted together reached out and intertwined with her and all she wanted was to give herself up.

We her family failed her because we could neither know nor express what it had been like to hold her dying husband in her arms. In the end the best we could do was to be patient and wait, rather than try to give every platitude scientific credibility, and analyse her every gesture until it became meaningless.

In the year that had passed since his death, we had taken her out into the countryside onto paths that were both familiar and remote enough not to risk encountering others. Although she agreed to come with us only reluctantly, a purpose returned to her step that was absent at other times. For many who know too the depths of grief, walking is an experience by which we understand ourselves in relation to the world. Through it the griever finds a security. While Marie-Jo was doing it mostly for our benefit, she seemed to rest more easily on her return from these excursions, as though, for a moment, she had been abandoned by her grief and was able to breathe more freely. Her friends and family still provided the scaffolding to support her, but over the months they had gradually returned to their own lives and could not be counted on to prop her up indefinitely. We hoped deeply that in these simple acts she would find a bulwark against the erosion of her own health, but when she returned home she would withdraw to the silence of her bedroom and the memories. She believed that if she let go of the one thing she had left, she would be cast from the only mooring that she had ever known.

Now that the summer was here again I had gone through my full wardrobe of running kit, from the shorts and singlets to the skin-tight tops that I wore through the winter in layers of three, together with my hat and gloves. Aside from learning to cope with the miles and the terrain, what I needed to prepare myself for was the heat of Greece at the height of the summer, where a year earlier temperatures had reached 42 degrees during the race. So I took to wearing black bin-liners under long-sleeved tops and on the hottest day of the English summer ran 20 miles up the river, wearing four layers, a woolly hat and sunglasses. I had never seen so much sweat pouring off me before, and when I got back home

I looked as if I had been pulled out of the river. I lost 4 kilos in one afternoon.

It was when she saw me like this that Laurence became most vocal about her fears for what I was putting myself through. My face had become gaunt; clothes that once fitted well now hung off me as though from a clothesline; and when I was lying in bed she could put her fingers right underneath my ribcage. However, it was not the fact that I had lost 10 kilos that worried her. In many ways she liked what I had become, but it was what I was doing to my heart that most troubled her. 'I have just lost my father,' she would remind me when I came back later than expected. 'I don't want to lose my husband.' The Spartathlon was now so close that I could look her in the eye and promise that it was nearly over. 'Never again, Robin. Never.'

Roman poets had a saying: 'solvitur ambulando' – anything could be worked out by walking, including one's own emotional tangles. In the twentieth century, Michel Foucault wrote that 'the country, by the gentleness and variety of its landscape, wins melancholics from their single obsession by taking them away from places that might revive the memory of the suffering'. Reaching across two millennia is a common idea that submitting ourselves to nature can restore our physical and mental health. 'Every day I walk myself into a state of wellbeing and walk away from every illness,' wrote the theologian and existentialist Søren Kierkegaard, while for

Robert Burton movement was the best cure for melancholy. Whether it is walking or running, motion has a meditative quality, an ability to slow down the rhythm of our lives, enabling us to regain an elemental foundation of self-knowledge and acceptance.

Those who have taken this logic to its extreme include Rosie Swale-Pope who, when she was widowed on her fifty-seventh birthday, set off to run around the world on her own. She covered almost the entire 21,000 miles across Europe, Russia, Siberia and North America unsupported, dragging along with her every possession she needed. It took her five years and fifty-three pairs of trainers.

Her husband had died of prostate cancer the year before and her aim, as expressed to those she met, was to raise money for charity. 'My run around the world started as a journey of loneliness, grief and heartbreak,' she writes. Hers may have been an extreme example, although as she had previously sailed around Cape Horn with her family and solo across the Atlantic, it was perhaps inevitably ambitious. But she understood, intuitively, that running was a way 'to find my way forward again'. She writes of wanting to give something back, of becoming conscious of her own mortality. Her husband's memory is written into every page. This was her way of grieving and of remembering him.

The transition from running marathons to distance races in which there is no measurement against the clock was starting to equip me with a new perception, a vigilant kind of looking, of the type that Iris Murdoch called 'attention [that] teaches us how real things can be looked at and loved without being seized and used, without being appropriated into the greedy organism of the self'. It restructures our attitude towards nature, making us more aware of people and the landscape, of tones and subtle changes. We become better attuned to our hopes and desires. Above all, we achieve patience in not trying to consume it whole, or pretending to have any kind of ownership over it. Through a return to nature we can live more authentically, feel less of a need to impose ourselves on it forcefully. Become calm again.

For Swale-Pope this moment came four years into her run as she crossed America. She writes simply that she had 'become the wildlife', having reached some kind of acceptance of her circumstances. In words that would echo with anyone coming to terms with loss, her final thoughts are familiar: 'Life is the greatest, happiest and often toughest adventure of all and I have fallen in love with it all over again.' Somewhere in that wilderness of grief she had come to accept what could not be altered and realised she had to move on.

It was exactly the experience that Richard Mabey describes in his recovery from depression, *Nature Cure*. 'My past, or lack of it, had caught up with me. I'd been bogged down in the same place for too long, trapped by habits and memories. I was clotted with rootlessness.' Mabey took himself back to what he loved in order to find himself again. The idea that he was propagating was to submit oneself to nature, to hope that it would 'take you out of yourself – dissolve the membrane between you and the world of health to which you belong'.

It is a story that Dean Karnazes, one of the most prominent ultra-distance runners in the world, would recognise. He is now so famous that Barack Obama jogged with him on a treadmill in Times Square for charity, although his first encounter with ultra-distance running came about late one night when he fled his own birthday party and just kept running.

He had been a good athlete at school, and it is clear that the desire to extend the limits of his endurance is part of his hard-wiring. He talks, as do all those who seek to enthuse others, of the human spirit being limitless and how all good things involve a struggle. However, that was not enough to prevent his being torn apart by the death of his sister in a car crash when she was a teenager. He ran 30 miles through that night, calling his wife in the morning, crying for help, an emotional wreck, his feet bleeding. 'And that's how I became a runner once again. In the course of a single night I had been transformed from a drunken yuppie fool into a re-born athlete. During a period of great emptiness in my life I turned to running for strength. I heard the calling, and went to the light . . . I reminded myself that pain and suffering are often the catalysts for life's most profound lessons.' Since that day he had run and won the 135-mile Badwater Ultra through Death Valley, and holds eleven Western State Silver buckles for sub-24-hour times in the 100-mile trail race.

Karnazes now tours the world, evangelising about the importance of good health and drawing metaphors for CEOs between the struggle on the trail and in the boardroom. In the end, though, he resorts to a quote from the existentialist novelist and goalkeeper Albert Camus to explain the privilege of the running experience: 'we are at home in our games because it is the only place we know what we are supposed to do.' I understood what Karnazes was getting at, as well as how hard it was to articulate for others. Running was not about racing or competition. It was about 'an education on the grace of living', as he put it, an education that taught him 'his place in the world'. It was a way of finding a peace that nature herself could teach us.

As I had come to realise myself, the illusion of our own empowerment over nature is embodied in the premise of home. It is when we measure ourselves against unshackled creatures such as Karnazes and Swale-Pope, for whom running is a way of life, that we realise just how much we define ourselves by the bricks and mortar that we build around our lives. Here we can construct our legacy and make permanent what we leave behind.

Armed with locked doors and the arbitrary boundaries of our garden fences, we deceive ourselves into thinking that we can control nature. With my mother-in-law in hospital, there was no one to cut the grass in her garden, and each time we returned to open up her house, I was amazed at how quickly nature had imposed itself again. The grass had migrated onto the patio and moss licked the window frame that only a month earlier we had cleaned. This was what the world would look like without us.

Jean-Louis and Marie-Jo had made a decision to establish themselves on the edge of a small market town deep in the French countryside, in part on behalf of the children they had yet to conceive. They built the house together, an architect coming from Paris with the plans, and there are photographs in the bathroom of the site rising up from the clay, one storey at a time. In the background are the young evergreens that would eventually grow together to form the perimeter of their world. This was the life they had chosen when they were not yet thirty and could see, with warm predictability, the decades opening up in front of them.

Theirs had been the first generation to break away to live far from their parents. A country so deceiving in its construct, France is really a collection of atomised particles and should never be one country at all. For Jean-Louis to move 200 kilometres north from his mother and father was to refute a law as immovable as gravity. Not for nothing had his two younger brothers moved barely an inch off the edge of the local map from the town where they had been born.

As the place my mother-in-law called home slowly disappeared under a scrub of suburban sadness, it became clear even a few months after she was widowed that she could not stay there. In that silence all she could hear was the clipping of his shoes on the stone stairs and the turning of a door handle that announced his presence. She could not stand it. Her purchase on the world around her became so brittle that it would take little more than a light breeze to separate her from it completely. Through that first year, as she retreated first to the house, then to her bedroom and sleep, we waited patiently for life to return, as though some other form of that previous existence was still possible.

We did not start to dismantle the house until after the first anniversary of his death. A vet came and bought all of Jean-Louis's surgical equipment and leftover stock. An entire history was boxed up and removed on a clattering trailer in a single afternoon. In the days that Laurence and I stayed in the house clearing up, the silence and the darkness that my mother-in-law had had to resist alone stared at us from every room. For the time being, the furniture remained, but it was clear that steps would eventually need to be taken to sell the house. It had long ago ceased to be a place of safety for Marie-Jo, and while she knew that she never wanted to go back, she could neither say where she did want to go. The very notion of home had evaporated for her.

'When it hurts,' wrote Czesław Miłosz, 'we return to the banks of certain rivers.' In the summer, at night, the river people of the Thames hooked electric torches to the masts of their boats. The breeze that gusted through trees made orange by the street lights carried the clinking sound of the lanterns against metal. On those evenings, out running after work, with the sound of traffic muffled by the solid canopy of leaves overhead, I imagined that I was looking at boatmen from another century.

The further I ran upstream, the denser the foliage along the banks became, until it turned so thick that it would flick back behind me as soon as I had passed through, obscuring the path I had taken. Sometimes I would have to keep my arms raised in front of me to crash through the overgrown branches. My battered feet, now reduced to layers of broken and blistered skin, the toenails having sloughed off and darkened, had become so used to this rugged path that I felt I knew every stone that I stepped on and I was almost skimming across the surface, barely touching the ground at all. By that summer I had finally learnt the kind of ergonomic rhythm that I had seen in those ultra athletes I had run with. I was now one of them.

So absorbed could I become in the density of what was around me — at times not being able to see more

than a few feet in front of me – that I would forget
where I was supposed to be going, or even that I was
running at all. Far enough upstream, the sound of the
aeroplanes bound for Heathrow disappeared altogether,
and it felt as if I had vanished into an age that pre-dated
modernity.

In 1947 the Conservators of the Thames fathered the
notion of the Thames River Walk. A route was agreed
and local authorities were approached to discuss the
division of costs. Between 1963 and 1964 the idea was
finally realised. Through the summer I was now running
up to 120 miles a week along this path, never tiring of
the scenery that was now flooded with light, as June
became July and then August and I counted down the
weeks until the Spartathlon. One weekend I took the
train out from Battersea to Windsor and ran the 40 miles
home, got up the next day and did it again.

We can learn more about ourselves in a single journey
along the Thames than we can across the oceans of the
world, as Peter Ackroyd says, because water reflects. In
the months after Jean-Louis's death, the frustration of
not being able to do anything to help my mother-in-
law was expunged from me. The further upstream I ran,
the more I became immersed in a kind of wild madness,
nature taking fully hold of me. I had never felt so alive,
so close to the 'Universal Eye' that Emerson wrote about
in *Nature*.

The Latin verb *cogito*, 'to think', has its etymology in

the idea of 'shaking things together', and when we run, additional oxygen is pumped through our brains as our bloodflow increases, feeding the imagination. When there is nothing more complicated to focus on than putting one foot in front of the other, the mind goes to work on unresolved problems. In the incommunicability of my own pain, I felt I better understood Marie-Jo's grief. After 20, 30, 40 miles, I would return home, mellow with a deep peacefulness, convinced that, with time, we would nurse her back to health. I felt full of purpose and clarity, as though I now knew that there would be a future for her. At the very least it was more productive than demolishing a bottle of gin, as I had done the day I had returned to London after the funeral. I came to believe that part of her restoration to health required that she witness nature's divinity first-hand, the ripple of the water, the dipping of the oar. This was the world that had cured Richard Mabey. This was the world that I wanted to submit her to, along with the science, as a path to restoration.

There is no better guide to the Thames, or to nature, than J. M. W. Turner, who spent a lifetime paddling up and down its length, from its pure source to its bubbling mass at Battersea. The river was 'wound around his soul', crucial for both his sense of self and his sense of the country. He 'understood its language', Ruskin declared.

For the runner along the Thames, Turner's paintings are essentially maps of the act of looking – an image of the point at which the artist comes into contact with the world in which he moves. His sketches are not just views of places, but documents of contemplation and comprehension, and they record the pace of a different century, a way of relating to things that we have come to forget. To learn from Turner and then take to the Thames armed with his knowledge is to be reminded that we are in many ways explorers in a foreign land, where there are still great stretches of water that are completely unpopulated, and where change occurs very slowly.

However, Turner cautioned that there was a limit to what he could do and what he wanted to do for his viewer. To experience nature in its totality means going to find it ourselves, and his landscapes were meant more as a reminder of what was out there than a substitution for the experience itself. His watercolours are washed out, the sky and the water having become one, in scenes familiar to us all from April showers. To rediscover what this is really like we have to go out and let the water run between our fingers. But the message is loud and beckoning across the centuries: in retreating to the safety of the clear, unpolluted water, Turner's river can become ours too.

The more I ran along Turner's banks, the more I became aware of a striking immediacy to the way in which I could feel the muddy world beneath me through my feet. Getting further and further out of London, up to Windsor, Henley and then, once, almost to the outskirts of Oxford, I believed that with just one more mile I would be able to capture that world fully, and return with it to my ordinary life. If this was a kind of madness, it was of the most tranquil kind in which I had fully given myself up to my watery surroundings. If only my mother-in-law could feel their tenderness and see what I had learnt to see, I was sure that her will to live would be restored. It was only when my phone rang and Laurence asked me where on earth I had got to that I would remember that I had promised to be home hours ago. I would lie, saying I was nearly home when in fact I was 20, sometimes 30 miles away. Then the moment would be lost, and I would feel as though I had been returned from a dream and I would have to stand still for a moment, figuring out how I was going to get home.

With that harmony came an unquantifiable yearning for solitude and silence, something that was near impossible when the modern life is defined by interaction. Running – and running here – was the only way that I could be left alone. To return to Turner's Thames was a means of escaping the perpetual noise of everyday life and finding space to think. Anyone can come down to the river bank and experience this world first-hand. This is what Turner has taught us, and what the runner can teach us too. It is not about knowledge or athleticism – not about isolated lights in a dark void of ignorance. This relationship is about sensuality – the sensation of the world at one's fingertips, once the clutter of twenty-first-century living has been abandoned.

In all the years that I had been running until I had started to question why I ran at all, once, maybe twice, I had experienced that ergonomic perfection in which feet, legs, body and swinging arms feel in harmony with the ground. But here, at last, I could summon it at will. Now, every time I came down to the river I would breathe in the fresh, crisp air, and it would heighten my senses to a level of almost peyotic preciseness, and I felt that I was aware of the world right down to the atomic level.

Before there was mass commercialisation of the sport, Emil Zátopek and Roger Bannister had run in plim-solls, and Abebe Bikila barefoot. The change to the modern running shoe began in 1962, when the Nike co-founder Bill Bowerman created the most cushioned running shoe ever seen – the Cortez.

The idea that Bowerman brought to his running shoe came from the observation that all previous great runners had run in exactly the same way, with their backs straight, their knees bent and their feet scratching back and forth directly under their hips, since the only way to absorb any shock was through the thick pad of the midfoot. What, Bowerman wondered, if you protected the heel from the impact? Could runners extend their stride and gain a little extra distance by stepping ahead of their centre of gravity? With the heel protected, the runner could adapt a heel-to-toe stride that straightened the legs and would therefore be less tiring over long distances. Where Bowerman led, others soon followed, with the running-shoe industry quickly hitting $1 billion in annual sales.

But the industrialisation of running has not been to everyone's taste. There are many who see the trainer as hindering the ergonomics of the runner and being the cause of many of the runner's physical ailments. Some runners have rebelled against the commercialisation of their sport by returning to what they call 'our natural state' to learn how to run all over again. A community has developed amongst ultra-distance athletes that advocates a return to the kind of running that our distant ancestor, *Homo erectus*, would have enjoyed – barefoot running. 'Running shoes may be the most destructive force to ever hit the human foot,' according to Dr Daniel Lieberman, a professor of biological anthropology at Harvard University. 'A lot of foot and knee injuries that are currently plaguing us are actually caused by people running with shoes that actually make our feet weak, cause us to over-pronate, give us knee problems.'

According to a study led by Bernard Marti, MD, a preventative-medicine specialist at Switzerland's University of Berne: 'There's no evidence that running shoes are any help at all in injury prevention ... Runners wearing top-of-the-line shoes are 123 per cent more likely to get injured than runners in cheap shoes.' By shielding our feet from the position in which we would normally run, barefoot, across the sand – up on the toes, the heel hardly touching the ground at all – we expose ourselves to unnecessary risk. Every year between 65 and 80 per cent of runners suffer an injury. No matter what size you are or shape you are in, the odds are the same. As Dr Gerard Hartmann explained: 'Putting your feet in shoes is similar to putting them in a plaster cast. If I put your leg in plaster, we'll find 40–60 per cent atrophy of the musculature within six weeks. Something similar happens to your feet when they're encased in shoes.'

But science, for some, has turned against this intuition. For some, the evidence pointing to the fact that, as creatures of the savannah, we are naturally inclined to run barefoot is irrelevant, since we have been clothed and shod for too long to effectively retrain those instincts. The researchers themselves seem to concede this point, concluding in their paper for *Nature* only that 'barefoot runners can run easily on the hardest surfaces in the world without discomfort from landing. If impacting transient forces contribute to some forms of injury, then this style of running (shod or barefoot) might have some benefits, but that hypothesis remains to be tested.'

The most famous barefoot runner of recent years is the South African Zola Budd, who still covers 10–15 miles, barefoot, every day. A growing number of British runners are following her example, albeit twenty years later, if not by going barefoot, at least by wearing foot 'gloves'. My feet had led me to the river and I concentrated hard on opening all my senses to nature. If I had had the courage, I would have followed her example too, and run the Thames Path barefoot, as a way of taking my immersion in my surroundings to its natural conclusion. But I was too fearful of what I could not see – the parts of nature whose danger I had been fully protected from in my urban life. Protected as I was, I could still get close to the marrow of things and let the place wash over me.

However briefly, for those minutes, hours – even days – down by the river, I would detach myself from the increased velocity of events around me. The trade-off was a heightened sense of anxiety that comes when we feel that we are falling behind. In this world, which I inhabited in parallel since I was still bound by the obligations of my daily life, if someone had come looking for me they would not have found me.

The etymology of 'lost' is the Old Norse *los*, meaning the disbanding of an army, suggesting a truce with the wider universe. If we are lost, we can also be at home in the unfamiliar, reading the landscape with new eyes, forced to search for patterns that will make us feel as though we belong. For Walter Benjamin, to get lost was to become, simply, 'fully present', to become fully immersed in uncertainty and mystery.

Virginia Woolf too deliberately went out to get lost in order to sharpen the sense that she was not tethered to a single perspective, that she could release herself from her moorings and not fear the consequences. The more I came to the river, the more I wanted to submerge myself in that naturalism, and in so doing show my mother-in-law that there was nothing to fear. I wanted to smell more deeply the sapling trees, to hear as precisely as possible the hum of insects, and then to bring a part of that nature back to her so that she could start to feel it for herself before venturing out to experience it first-hand.

Over those last weekends of training, when it seemed as though I returned home only to eat and sleep before setting off to run again, I found that I could more easily trace the natural landscape that Turner had seized and called his own. The acceptance of my own limitations, both as an individual and as a runner, brought me as close as I could possibly get to achieving the desired harmonious existence with this watery world: an existence in which I passed over it, rather than imposed myself upon it. It even got to the point where the miles I covered were no longer about training for the Spartathlon but instead had become about the moment itself. It was only when I arrived at the entrance of the gym, teeth clenched in adolescent petulance for having been forced there against my will, that I would remember why I had started this journey in the first place.

Looking back, as Cherry-Garrard had done from the warmth of his living room, I wonder now whether this was the time when something within me, if not broke, then certainly bent, the obsession with running turning into something beyond my control. Every day was constructed around running, and when I was not some-where along the Thames, I was in the gym for up to 2 hours at a time. After each session, clanking weights, heaving medicine balls around, balancing precariously to do even more elaborate sit-ups, I would descend to the sauna and sit for 20, 25, 30 minutes at a time, barely breathing. Not because it was doing me any good – I can see that now – but because I could. I would then return home too exhausted to speak and would retreat to bed before it was even dark, falling immediately into a deep dreamless sleep. In the morning Laurence would shake me awake and I would beg for just 5 more minutes in bed.

In that year I also fell away from many people I had known nearly my whole life. Perhaps I was asking too much of them, just as I had expected too much of them when Jean-Louis had died, thinking that we would grow close again as they took from us whatever burden of grief friendship was capable of. I realised too late that I was as much at fault as they were. I too should have been concentrating on saving up for a car or increasing my mortgage payments, because when we met up, less and less frequently, after the first effusion there was an increased awkwardness between us. The conversation would stop and we would have to search for a subject to begin it again. In the end it seemed that we had agreed, without wanting to embarrass the other by acknowledging it, not to meet up again. And when we did see each other at parties, we would be careful to talk only when others were present for fear that the embarrassment would resurface.

I must take some responsibility for this as well since I had now become so consumed by getting ready for the Spartathlon that I could talk of little else. At parties I would explain to anyone who listened just what I was planning to do. From across the room I could see Laurence watching me to be sure that I was not boring people. Some of them would nod, in the way that signals that the topic of conversation had run its course, pointing out that I had never looked so lean, that my skin was glowing with health. Both observations were true, but were such insignificant consequences of what I was putting myself through that I would use them as an excuse to start talking about the race all over again. I would get annoyed when people asked why I was doing it at all, frustrated that they could not see that, by asking why, they were questioning my very reason for being. Sometimes I got so wound up that I would leave the party early and wait on the pavement until Laurence was ready to go home.

And it was not just with friends that I lost my focus. Back in the office on Monday mornings I would feel that I was still out there by the river, not yet having quite reconnected with the world of other people. I would sit through meetings, listening, as though through water, to what took place around me. So distracted would I sometimes get that I would strap my heart-rate monitor to my chest during presentations, watching my heart rate fall from 40 to 38, then 36, and once to 31 beats per minute as I slowed my breathing. It was the only thing I could do to keep my attention focused in the room, since all I could hear was the birdsong and the sucking of the river along the banks in a spectrum of delight.

With the solitude of those hours came a better empathetic understanding of what Sara Maitland calls in *A Book of Silence* the 'interior dimension of silence – stillness of the heart and the mind', akin to the same four walls that enclosed my mother-in-law every day. The mounting sense of resolution that I experienced over these days and then weeks came from finally starting to understand what it was like to suffer without language to communicate it fully. But the transformation that she had to undergo would happen only when she decided that she wanted to see this world too.

We returned to France every few weeks. Although enough time had elapsed for us to realise that there would be no silver bullet, there came with each passing day a mounting faith, born out of acceptance, that, if she had got this far, then she would come through her grief. There would be a future after all.

The inevitable creep of civilisation, which Turner spent his life fighting so hard against, was manifested in the late 1830s when the Great Western Railway opened up the upper reaches of the Thames. The hulking wrecker, travelling at a fantastical 50 miles an hour, had no regard for the river's melodic existence. As Turner's reputation diminished from greatness into sentimentality, so the river ceased to be a measure of the natural pace of things. If there is one place that symbolises the transition from old to new, it is at Maidenhead where Brunel's bridge, consisting of two enormous brick arches, was constructed to carry passengers from London. Those who now wrote Turner off as a romantic did so too quickly. It was here, in 1844, that he took a deep breath and embraced the modern sciences of physics and geometry, to paint *Rain, Steam and Speed*, his most famous lament about the brave new world that had left him behind.

'Railway mania' became a fashionable subject for painters in the 1830s and 1840s, although many merely conveyed the prosaic mechanics of the railway engine or the grandeur of the landscape it could conquer. However, in *Rain, Steam and Speed*, Turner takes us back to the four elements of the modern age — rain, steam, speed and the Great Western Railway — and succinctly grades their status to reflect the social changes that the railway had brought.

If you stand before the painting, at first nothing is grasped fully, except that the modern viewer is now apparently moving so fast that he has lost all contact with nature. The story of the railway that emerges stands for the complete negation of all that Turner valued and stood for, since anyone travelling through life at this pace would have nothing whatsoever to show for the experience of their journey.

Water pervades the painting, almost engulfing both the train and the bridge, as the passengers fly over the river in the rain. Fire heats the water to make the steam as the train flashes across the canvas, while the angelic figures, represented by fishermen in their skiffs, can only wave at it from below, the speed of a mechanised society having far overtaken them. Earth is represented here too in the figure of the lonely ploughman, low down on the right, labouring with the old technology, trudging hopelessly through the filthy weather in the opposite direction. For each and every one, as for Turner, this new age is not for them.

I went looking for this world at Maidenhead, maybe forcing the vision too strongly to see what Turner had really seen, since, for the runner, the creep of London's civilisation starts only when the Thames path turns from grass at Windsor to cobbles at Teddington Lock and to tarmac at Putney Bridge. Alongside this metamorphosis, the energy of the river changes too, from agriculture and pastoral pleasure to politics and commerce. Through the last wending of the river, it widens dramatically into full maturity. Now the sea beckons, with motorised boats polished for Bank Holiday weekends; the bridges evolve from stone to steel, outdoing even Brunel. In this transition, Turner's river hands over to that of Dickens, who lived at Gad's Hill and had only to gaze into his glowing fireplace on New Year's Eve to feel such ghostly 'incidents of travel arise round me from all the latitudes and longitudes of the Globe'. It was his ghosts who stalked the waters here as, lest we forget, *Our Mutual Friend* starts with the bodysnatcher and his daughter Lizzie, floating 'on the Thames, between Southwark Bridge which is of iron, and London Bridge which is of stone, as an autumn evening was closing in'.

For Dickens, the Thames was essentially a river of tears and darkness, carrying with it the pollution of the macabre side of humanity. Joseph Conrad, who could for comparison draw on the sickly air of Africa, called it 'one of the dark places on earth'. Whilst Conrad had sailed the Thames's distant reaches, his 'faithful river' was confined to the section that once led to the densely clustered warehouses of the London docks. His vision was shaped entirely by a working knowledge of the estuary, its shifting sands, currents and winds. This was the imperial river of the nineteenth century, a 'waterway leading to the uttermost end of the earth', as Marlow said in *Heart of Darkness*. For the French novelist Céline, the experience of the docks of London was like walking into an earthquake. If ever there was a reminder that our responsibilities as runners were foremost about being human, and that our escape from them was only ever temporary, it washes up here on the banks of the same river.

While nothing had changed, and my prolonged absence had not been noted, at least I knew now that running teaches us patience and with that comes compassion – the knowledge of how to become properly grounded, more accepting. And when the understanding did come of what running was really about, it was not in a moment of deep reflection, but in one of complete exhaustion, with my body given over to it in its entirety. I knew now that there was no point in getting frustrated with my inability to articulate more clearly the joy that it gave me. I had to accept that the pleasure was a deeply subjective, if also universally achievable, state of grace.

The ultra-distance elite runners that I had come to know were all driven by an urge that could manifest itself in many forms. Starting lines were filled with recovered alcoholics, veterans of multiple marriages, individuals who came to long-distance running as a means of exhausting the tic that had broken them when it had shown itself in another, more destructive, form.

It might appear counter-intuitive to ask what ultra-distance runners can teach us about how to live, since they are almost impossible to track down and rarely commit their words to the page for the rest of us to learn by. Although this has changed in recent years – Karnazes' autobiography was a best-seller, as was Chris McDougall's *Born to Run* – for these athletes, running is their legacy, and what gnomic advice they can give can be put in full context only when we take to the road ourselves.

Amongst the most mystical of ultra-distance runners is Scott Jurek, who won the Spartathlon in three consecutive years from 2006. Those who have heard him talk rarely ask him why he does it, knowing that it is not a straightforward question, and have instead focused on his stories of adventure and pain, which any running audience appreciates. In the few explanations he has given of the life that he leads, he has never cited Thoreau as an inspiration, nor suggested that he was aware of the lines from *Walden* that told of heading to the woods to 'live more deliberately'. Yet this is exactly the life that Jurek has chosen.

There is a website that purports to keep fans in touch with Jurek's running schedule, but so frequently does he disappear off the map that the site is regularly anything up to six months out of date. The journalist Chris McDougall eventually managed to track him down for a book he was writing about the Tarahumara tribe in Mexico, who are believed to be the best natural runners in the world. McDougall wanted to find out whether this was true and to make the comparison asked Jurek whether he would come and race them. Although the book is about the Tarahumaras, Jurek appears only moments before the race, consistently vanishing just when McDougall thinks he has got him to commit, making the quest for understanding why he runs as heroic a failure as the hunt for Moby Dick. The one-line explanation for why he runs comes in a quote from William James: 'beyond the extreme of fatigue and distress, we may find amounts of ease and power we never dreamed ourselves to own; sources of strength never taxed at all because we never push through the obstruction.'

Even Jurek, though, is not immune to the turbulence of everyday life. By 2008 he had won almost every ultra-distance race in the calendar, but within a year his wife, a non-runner, had left him and though he was still running and still winning, he was starting to wonder how much longer he was going to be able to carry on.

'I think he's always been a conflicted guy,' McDougall says. 'I think he's always struggled to figure out who he is and what he should do. I think the success came by accident and the clarity was never there. I think he started to win and he thought, Oh, this is who I am. I think [now] . . . he's not winning and he's wondering who he is. Scott always felt that if he stuck to the pure way, the Zen way, the art of the warrior way, he would get everything he wanted. His approach was, you get out there, you run the races and win the races. You tackle all the hard races and you dominate them, then in the end you will be the hero. And what he found is the opposite. He raced everyone. Everyone! From Greeks on their home course to the Tarahumara Indians in Mexico to winning Badwater and Western States [races] within two weeks of each other. And what did he get? His wife left him. He lost his best friend. No huge endorsements. So no, I don't think he has that clarity of purpose any more.'

And with the fragility of greatness comes self-doubt, but also the answers to why Jurek does keep going. 'I've definitely done it more pure, but that's the way I was raised. Prove yourself by getting out and doing it . . . I'm more of the mind – do it and they will come to you.'

Then comes the question of his own legacy. 'I keep wondering why I'm going back,' he says. 'Maybe for getting a glimpse of my soul. At the moment, though, I'm hitting the pain and discomfort. That's where you have to think about guts, or spirit, or the soul. Something more than the mind or body.' Anyone who thinks that to be able to run faster and further than anyone else is about winning is missing the point, he says. 'It's not about money. It's not even about suffering, or redemption. It's about discovery. It's about finding one's path. It's about using experience in life to shape something completely different. That's the art of living.'

Emerson could have had Jurek in mind when he wrote: 'the lover of nature is he whose inward and outward senses are still truly adjusted to each other; who has retained the spirit of infancy even into the era of manhood.' Jurek's way of running is a return to the wild, not as a means of negating civilisation but as a way of reminding himself of the world that exists without him, to feel fully humbled before its beauty. He exists as an individual apart from nature, but can sense its beauty at the atomic level, and he understands what it means to be a part of it. And this is the moment when the clarity of purpose returns to Jurek.

Although now he gets injured more often, pulling out of races because of the pain that, before, he could not give a name to, he is calm again. What Jurek can teach us is that the transformation we undergo in becoming ultra-distance runners involves a merging of consciousness and landscape, whilst offering up the possibility of going beyond the limits of our knowledge. The transformation is in the act of running itself, which turns running from a mode of travel – in its most limited form, of getting across the finish line – to a mode of being.

7

The Journey to the End of the Night

It took me two weeks to pack my bags for Greece. I measured and weighed layers of clothes, folded and unfolded my running kit, and packed and repacked everything before we left for the airport. Through four seasons the One Great Project had finally ripened. Thirty-six hours! Non-stop! Impossible!

I returned to the maps of the Peloponnese again and again, as I knew all the competitors were doing, to trace with my finger the contours we were going to cover. The maps made me feel like a professional as they revealed the points of strengths and weakness in my assault. It was as though they were the blueprints to a bank that I was about to rob. But it seemed to be no use, as with time they simply revealed more clearly the insurmountability of the challenge. My imagination could not hold the thought for long. As Melville wrote in *Moby Dick*: 'It is not down in any map; true places never are.' I would put away the maps, as the twisted paths and dotted lines silently mocked me. And here was the paradox: I was preparing to annihilate myself, to cut myself off from all I knew and to retreat from progress – the path of normality – and then I would try to revert to language to communicate the experience.

Every detail had found its place in the notebook I had kept through the year: speeds, distances covered, weight lost and gained. There were also training plans, dietary requirements, logged times, sketches of the races to compete in as preparation. I had worked out the skeleton of an itinerary that covered everything from how to treat my feet before my shoes went on, to what time to arrive at the start line and what food to eat as I ran. Over the course of the race there were seventy-two numbered water stations, roughly 4 kilometres apart, where I would leave bags with dates, nuts, goji berries, fruit pastilles and carbohydrate powder. One water bottle would be strapped to my back, a heart-rate monitor to my chest and a speed monitor to my belt. There would also be a mobile phone, sunglasses and a sunhat. There would be a head torch waiting for me at the 109-kilometre checkpoint for the night section, with a change of socks and a fluorescent jacket. Every conceivable eventuality was committed to paper, leaving nothing to chance. Each sentence was an attempt to secure a final logic against the inevitable deterioration of body and mind. Yet this was as far as the science could go. No amount of preparation could tell me what 36 hours on my feet would *feel* like.

Deep within me I knew that I had no earthly business thinking that I could take on the 152 miles, even though on the two preceding Sundays I had run my fastest marathons ever, taking 20 minutes off my previous best times, getting round in 3:12. Since its conception in 1984, no more than 700 people have ever completed the Spartathlon. To emphasise just how tough this race was, I remembered that even those who did not finish were serious ultra-distance runners, since the minimum criterion for qualification was completing a 100-kilometre race in under 10½ hours. These were the best ultra-distance runners in the world.

I arrived in Athens ten days before the race, like a thief disguised as a late-summer holidaymaker, with the tools of my heist passing unnoticed through the security checks. The outrageous idea of thinking that, after twelve months, I was able to line up on the start line of the toughest endurance race in the world, had kept me prisoner for a year. The word 'impossible' still reverberated around my skull and at times I wondered what I had gotten myself into by shackling myself to this ridiculous idea. Part of me almost hoped that I would be found out, detained immediately and sent back home where I belonged.

On the plane I had been reading Philippe Petit's account of the high-wire crossing he made between the Twin Towers in New York. The passenger next to me told me she had just seen his film, *Man on Wire*. She asked whether I had come to Athens for a holiday. I replied theatrically, '25 September, 7 a.m. at the Acropolis,' mimicking Petit's cryptic allusion to his act. She stared at me blankly and the joke fell flat as she turned away without asking what I meant.

Laurence and I took a boat to one of the islands and for a week I jogged on the beach, acclimatising to the heat. Every day I would wake to watch the Mediterranean sunrise, thinking forward to the moment that we would stand at the foot of the Acropolis. As the temperature rose during the day, I understood that if I could get past 3 p.m. and the worst of the heat, then I might have a chance.

We did calculations on the back of restaurant napkins, showing how fast I needed to run to get to Corinth in the required 9½ hours. Each morning in the sea I cleaned, filed and sanded down my feet to make sure that there was no loose skin or hard surfaces that would be exposed to abrasions. At home, friends were planning families and organising the next stages in their lives. 'Don't think that I don't understand,' Laurence said. 'You want to do something extraordinary. I see that. But just once, then enough. We have a life to get on with, and I don't want to do that alone.'

My meticulous plotting had almost been foiled in the final week before I left for Greece by the doctor from whom I had to get a letter passing me as fit to run the race. I had understood this to be a formality since, like all other participants, I had already agreed that I was taking full responsibility for my safety. But as the doctor held the stethoscope to my chest for far longer than seemed necessary, he declared that he could hear a 'systolic murmur loudest in the left parasternal region', and he wouldn't sign the letter. I was *too* fit. My resting heart rate had dropped to 31 beats per minute and each beat was followed by a whooshing noise as the chambers filled with blood.

The murmur is a phenomenon that is common among professional athletes, and he was unsurprised to have found it, but could not be sure that it was not a pathological sign of a problem with my arteries. I would have to have an ultra-sonic scan and an ECG, then see the cardiologist.

With three days to go until I flew to Athens, I lay in the Royal Brompton Hospital as the cardiographer built an ultrasound picture of my heart between my ribcage, my diaphragm and through my throat to get behind the breastbone. Twelve hours later I sat in the cardiologist's office, counting up the cost of what one piece of paper was worth as I was subjected to a lecture on why ultra-distance running had long-term damaging effects on the body. I was told that Sebastian Coe's ECG results were held up to medical students as reason to think that long-distance running 'almost inevitably causes cardiac problems including atrial fibrillation, left ventricular hypertrophy with consequent diastolic heart disease and sometimes block'. I assured the cardiologist that this was a one-off and he nodded in paternal satisfaction.

'The human body is not designed to run long distances,' he said, contradicting almost every scientific text that I had read. I said nothing, thinking instead that humankind had not been designed to land on the moon. The following morning I had my piece of paper.

On the afternoon before the race, I arrived at the Hotel London in Athens for final registration. The lobby was full of emaciated men and a few women, agitating between sofas like mosquitoes. Some were already dressed in their running kit, excitably talking in languages that I could place but not understand. There was only one thing to say: we are finally here. This is where the logic of wanting to run a marathon really ends: with 400 of the best ultra-distance runners in the world crammed into a one-star hotel on a busy motorway. Everyone knew that less than 30 per cent of us would finish, but for the time being that was all ahead of us. We were still invincible.

The weathered faces of the runners, mostly in their forties and fifties, told of years rather than months spent on the road. Bare feet revealed sock-level tan lines, and deep grooves around the eyes spoke of hours gazing transfixed at the horizon. The age of these runners indicated that they had tired of marathons. It also suggested the maturity required to spend this amount of time on your feet. All but the elite need two or three attempts to finish the Spartathlon, and after each race those who do not finish come back the following year, wiser and stronger and with a determination not to be broken this time.

They were not professional athletes, since the Spartathlon prides itself in not offering any cash prize to the winner. The competitors are the people who guard your prisons, put out your fires, decorate your homes and deliver your post. They are humble, quiet and ordinary, for whom running is a deeply personal, introspective pursuit. For many it is not a pastime but a way of life. Wives and girlfriends, husbands and children followed dutifully behind in specially made T-shirts, displaying their unwavering loyalty.

The average age of the runners, many of whom scheduled their entire annual holiday allowance around racing, also suggested that, for many, undertaking this Herculean task was a form of rebellion against growing old and the established order of things. For most of them the only sense of competition was running against the clock and to finish was enough.

As the months had progressed and my training runs had become longer and greater in number, I had frequently asked myself what sort of game I was playing. No one really wanted me to do this, least of all Laurence with everything that had happened in the last year. In fact everyone I knew said that it was an extremely bad idea. At thirty-two I too should have been acting like a responsible adult rather than still be looking for ways to rebel against the corridors of convention that had lined my childhood. If these runners knew that the strain these distances were putting on their hearts over so many years had made them prone to 'cardiac problems including atrial fibrillation, left ventricular hypertrophy with consequent diastolic heart disease and sometimes block', they were not showing it. They had no intention of going quietly.

Looking lost in the hotel lobby, I was befriended immediately by Gilles, a French veteran of ten Spartathlon finishes. He put his arm around my shoulder when I told him it was my first time and smiled. 'La première fois c'est très dure!' Gilles had run fourteen 200-kilometre races since April and he made it clear that, with less than 24 hours until the start, a competitor's success or failure was predetermined by a training plan that dated back as far perhaps as Christmas Day. All these runners knew it and there was nothing that any of us could do now except stand around and wait.

Gilles said that he planned every holiday around running races, 'the cheaper the better', and spent his entire year training for the Spartathlon, the purest running race in the world and the hardest. The rest, especially the Marathon des Sables, was 'pour les frimeurs', show-offs. The latter was not even that tough, since it took place over six days with time to sleep between stages. The Spartathlon, by contrast, is a deliberately fast race with strict time limits for leaving each of the seventy-two checkpoints. For some the greatest hurdle is the heat, for others it is running through the night, but for every competitor there is no possibility of stopping, no time to compose yourself if it starts going wrong.

When the alarm went off at 4 a.m., I had already been awake for 2 hours. Under a cool autumnal sky, we walked the final 100 metres through the olive groves beneath the Parthenon, still lit up like a golden ark. Huddles formed as we gave one another one last shout of encouragement. Gilles wandered between the runners, wishing them all luck. He saw me as I walked to the back of the group to perform some futile last-minute stretches. He had thought my idea of running two 4½-hour marathons to Corinth, the first major checkpoint, a good one. 'Patience! Patience! Patience!' he said, raising his finger to emphasise the importance of his advice.

With 5 minutes to the bell, I felt that familiar fatigue take hold of my legs as though I was sinking into a warm bath. It had taken me a year to get here and I was in danger of overloading the moment with symbolism: that to be finally off would mark the neat closure of one part of my life. In my mind, the last year had been constructed out of straight lines and grids of regular shapes imposed regimentally on my daily routine. And now, in the morning haze, that was all about to be broken apart. I was thinking too far ahead; I was already in Sparta. For now the only thing that mattered was getting to Checkpoint 22 in Corinth, at 81 kilometres.

The bell rang and shouts of joy went up. Four hundred runners wested out of Athens down the steep slope of the Acropolis, as a weak sunlight stole over the landscape, like a thief through the window someone forgot to close. Like the last explorers in a mapped-out world, we were pioneers pushing back the boundaries so that those left behind could enjoy a sense of exploration in their own imaginations, but in the comfort of knowing that others had returned before them and shown that it could be done.

I was the last to cross the start line and gave one final wave to Laurence. All those miles that I had run through the year while she was grieving rose up at once, forcing us apart. The chasm between us seemed an obscene distance and I could not tell what she was thinking. I would not see her now until Sparta.

There is no neat equation that explains why people choose to put themselves through the trial of running these distances. For some, like Gilles and Thierry, with whom I ran for the first 7 hours, it was a way of releasing the coiled-up tension in a personality that was so tightly wound that to imagine them not running was to ask for trouble. For others, like Mark Cockbain, who arrived at the hotel with a bag slung over his shoulder as though for a beach holiday, running these distances exfoliated the junk of everyday life. But if there was one generalisation that seemed applicable to every runner as we stretched out through the suburbs of Athens, it was what Edward O. Wilson calls biophilia: a love of life.

Wilson understood that to be curious is the essence of what it is to be alive. In the world of the ultra-distance runner this sense of curiosity is felt deeply and positively, and to take on these challenges is a way for them to go beyond the boundaries of the everyday to enjoy a hypersensitive experience of the environment over which they are running, as well as of the terrain of the body as it gently crumbles away.

What we were anticipating, as we prepared to take our bodies to the limits of their capability, was what Arthur Koestler described in *The Act of Creation* as 'an upward surge from the unknown, fertile, underground layers of the mind'. This is the exhilaration of *feeling*, of the physical and emotional response to disintegration, and the point at which the mind empties itself of all habits. The result is the interlocking of previously unconnected matrices of thought and experience. Unconnected ideas, quite literally, are shaken together. And out of that creative act is generated a new topography of the individual and, by extension, the world.

The year that I had spent training for this race had not simply been about crafting a runner out of my body, it was also about learning the language with which to articulate the experience. Along with this knowledge came the warning from the ultra-distance runners that I had learnt from: that part of its meaning would be beyond language itself. The truly creative act often starts where language ends.

The road to Sparta had started with a simple question – why do we run? I had spent twelve months training for the race, but had also been trying to understand better what compelled me to do it. At its most public, we run for the competition and the adventure. However, the more I ran, the more I realised that for me it was a far more personal epiphany, anchored in pain and revelation, but even these motivations were difficult to fully grasp. Perhaps there is no answer that could be captured by language. This is just what we do, and running these distances offers a richness of experience that contributes to our understanding of not only ourselves but of the landscape and our own personal history. To be reductive is to miss the point, as it is the 'what', not the 'why' that matters. Regardless of how well I could convey what it was like to run this race, there would always be a gap between what it sounded like and what it felt like.

Behind me I saw it for the first time – daybreak. A cool, limpid sunrise, little more than a lightening of the eastern haze, a brief intensity of cloud that would evaporate within the hour. As the first hours passed, we ran against the flow of commuter traffic and through the bulging industrial estates on the outskirts of Athens, before turning off the motorway to weave along the old coastal road to Corinth. For most of the day I ran with Thierry. Because of his knowledge of the race, he knew to wear earplugs to keep out the noise of the traffic, and perhaps also to lock himself into a space in which he could hear only the metronomic beat of his own rhythm. The heat did not start to become uncomfortable until midday, but those, like Gilles and Thierry, who had been here many times before, knew what effect it could have and wore the least amount of kit possible.

I was reminded of the time when I had been on the plane to fly out for the Athens Marathon. Clothed, these men looked startlingly humble. You might walk right through them on any other day. We can see the true strength of someone only when they are stripped down, at which point these men suddenly became supermen. The sinews and muscles down the backs of their legs ricocheted with every step. Even with their arms hanging loosely down by their sides, each particle of tissue and muscle, sharply defined, flexed like rippling sheets with their every movement. I had never been this close to the sensuality of the athletic form before, but it was clear to see now what had drawn hundreds of thousands to the site of Olympia to worship the mortal form.

In all the time I spent with the runners of the Spartathlon, there was never any sign of the vanity acquired by the first-time marathon runner. All aesthetic perfection had long ago been put to one side, as though their physical manifestation as runners was incidental to their cognitive being.

'Take care of what happens up here,' Thierry said, tapping his temple with his index finger, as we slowed to a walk over the first climb. He explained that the body is little more than a vehicle for carrying the will. I looked at him doubtfully. 'All you need to do with the legs is more of this – boom, boom, boom,' he said, indicating the motion of running. 'When the mind starts to go, then you know you are finished.' With our heads to the wind, like a compass cleaving to the north, we stiffened and steadied ourselves, waiting for the gusts to die down.

Through that first day those who had raced before expended as little energy as possible, saving as much as they could for the night and the mountains that we still had to climb. The rest of us were distracted from what lay ahead by the beauty of the landscape around us, once we had parted company with the traffic outside Athens. In *The Colossus of Maroussi*, Henry Miller wrote: 'Greek light acquires a transcendental quality: it is not the light of the Mediterranean alone, it is something more, something unfathomable, something holy. Here the light penetrates directly to the soul, opens the doors and windows of the heart, makes one naked, exposed, isolated . . . no analysis can go on in this light; here the neurotic is either instantly healed or goes mad.' There was a magnificence to the scenery that even the filth of Athens, with its smog and its litter, could not ruin.

With the hottest part of the day, which peaked at 42 degrees, came the water as we joined the coastal road. To our right, white cliffs thrust away to a blue sky and to our left fell into a sea that breathed quietly, like a sleeping dog. I was not alone in yearning to strip off completely and plunge in headlong, and I passed a Japanese runner clutching an ice pack to his head while looking over the edge longingly. As focused as we each were on our own race, at the end of it all we were in this together. Until the 36 hours were up, his pain was our pain, his longing, ours too.

Paul was eighteen when he decided to become a priest. At university we had heard him leave for church through the stupor of Sunday mornings, but we had never expected this. The summer after our finals, he moved to Rome to embrace the intense loneliness of contemplation that I suspected the rest of us feared and so filled with the distraction of other people. In the six years that he spent there, our lives diverged completely. It was clear that he was to be tested by the awesomeness of his decision to pursue a spiritual life, to learn to be silent in a world of noise, and to discover that silence has no narrative. Silence intensifies sensation – by turning the body inwards. It was clear, too, that he wanted to be tested, to mortify the flesh through reflection, and to embrace wholly what the psychologist William James calls the essence of religion: the experience of solitude, understood in relation to whatever we may consider to be the divine.

The world that I had entered through long-distance running started as a simple geometrical relationship with the maps and the routes that would take us from the start to the finish line. In the intervening months it had transformed into an experience of intense solitude in which hours passed in silence, resulting in an increased hypersensitivity of both body and mind. I had not expected it, but I had come to see that to run was to know how to cope with that silence. To survive its rigours requires an interior peacefulness in which, as James wrote, we feel 'the keynote of the universe sounding in our ears, and everlasting possession spread before our eyes. The sort of happiness in the absolute and everlasting [that] we find nowhere but in religion.'

Twenty-seven years after the inaugural Spartathlon, no one has come within 1½ hours of Yannis Kouros's time of 20 hours and 25 minutes, set in 1984. When he won the inaugural race in 21:53.00 no one had ever heard of him and suspicions were raised that he had cheated by cadging a lift on the back of a motorcycle. He shrugged his shoulders and returned the following year to better his time, before turning around and running back to Athens.

Between 1984 and 1991, when he retired temporarily, he dominated ultra-distance racing. The records show races of 300+ kilometres, won by more than 3 hours, and the 1,060-kilometre Sydney to Melbourne race, won by more than 24 hours, in 134:47.00 hours. Not only is he fast over these distances, but he also requires virtually no sleep. In one 144-hour – or six-day – race he rested for less than 4 hours. While his body has changed shape, becoming progressively more muscular in the torso, trunk and legs, making him look more now like a mesomorphic wrestler than a runner, there are few physiological explanations for his success. Very little is known about his training regime, other than that he runs between 20 and 25 kilometres every day and, like Scott Jurek, is virtually a vegetarian. However, clues can be found in his meticulous pre-race preparation, which is spent listening to music to put him in what he calls 'a trance-like state'. This may explain why his greatest races have been on indoor tracks, closed road loops or open roads with no traffic, where his attention is not diverted and he can almost completely shut out the world.

Kouros has much in common with the Japanese monks who live high up on Mount Hiei, in a monastery founded in 1787, and have defined marathon running as a path to spiritual enlightenment through the renunciation of the flesh. According to John Stevens, who became a marathon monk, their way of life 'offers the seeker every type of religious experience: sacred scholarship, grand ritual, austere meditation, heartfelt repentance, heroic asceticism, mystical flight, miraculous cures, ceaseless devotion, divine joy, and nature worship – while promising enlightenment in this very body'. To become a monk at Mount Hiei requires a 100-day term of *kaihogyo*, the 'practice of circling the mountains'. Each candidate is given a white outfit to wear and a rope to tie around his waist, which holds a knife for him to use to commit suicide if he cannot complete the term.

Each day, the apprentice begins at midnight and must cover 40 kilometres before returning between 7 and 9 a.m. to attend a service, bathe and eat a midday meal. This routine is repeated for 100 days and must also include a 54-kilometre run accompanied by one of the senior priests. By the seventieth day, the apprentice will have 'acquired the marathon monk stride: eyes focused about 100 feet ahead while moving along in a steady rhythm, keeping the head level, the shoulders relaxed, the back straight, and the nose and navel aligned'. If he is successful, he can petition to try the 1,000-day term, which takes seven years to complete. The final year of the 1,000-day term consists of two 100-day terms of daily 84-kilometre runs to be completed every day within 16 to 18 hours. Only then is that runner declared to be a Daigyoman Ajari, a 'Saintly Master of the Highest Practice'. Since 1885, only forty-six monks have completed the training.

After the 700th day, the apprentice must learn to face death by surviving nine days without food, water, sleep or rest, at the end of which he 'becomes one with the mountain, flying along a path that is free of obstruction'. He acquires a new sensitivity to life and 'can hear ashes fall from incense sticks, smell and identify foods from miles away and see the sun and moonlight seep into the interior of the temple'.

In *The Varieties of Religious Experience*, William James wrote: 'at bottom the whole concern of both morality and religion is with the manner of our acceptance of the universe. Do we accept it only in part and grudgingly, or heartily and altogether?' If we accept it, we no longer wish to escape, but instead take our place in the divine order of things. For these monks, who were found after seven years to show many of the indications usually associated with a dead body, asceticism is a means of turning flesh into The Word.

Although I hesitate to push the metaphor too far, to be running the Spartathlon was the closest I could come to the religious experience that Paul had set out to acquire.

The mood at Corinth – where Thierry sat down in the shade and tore open a sachet of rehydration powder, dismayed by his body's failure to deal with the heat – carried me through the rest of the day. Thierry shook his head when I asked whether he was carrying on. I tried to resist the feeling that I might actually be born to this kind of running since I was outlasting someone who had done it twelve times before. I knew that the longer I had someone to run with, even if we just moved along together in silence, the easier it would be to hold myself together.

Fifty of those who had set off ahead of me in Athens had handed in their numbers by the time I left Checkpoint 22. I was surprised to find that although my swollen feet ached and my legs had warmed to that feeling of pleasant discomfort, there was nothing in the muscles yet that was telling me to stop. The evening sun endowed rocks and dust particles with thousands of voices, and I remembered with great joy the summer, ten years previously, that Paul and I had spent wandering around Italy and Greece, along these same paths. Feeling unavoidably sentimental about the intervening years, I could not help but recall it as a time of immense happiness, when the aching heart that comes with irrevocable loss and the bitterness of mistakes was still far distant in the future.

With Corinth behind us and the first psychological barrier having winnowed out the day's weakest runners, a greater distance began to stretch between those who were left. Occasionally a runner would pass me, nod and carry on. By the time I reached the next checkpoint, they had already either moved on or given up. By 8 p.m. the remaining light had faded completely. Most of us had yet to pick up our night gear so we had to grope along as best we could. This was true dusk, a thick gloom that blended into the rock as if it had been cast there like a blanket. As we travelled through the last villages before moving closer to the mountains, young children had run out to us asking for our autographs. Whole books were filled with the names of those who had passed through hours or even years ago. I wondered whether they were taking everyone's signature to hedge their bets about who was going to get through the night at all.

Occasionally a car would pass by, stirring up dust particles disturbed by runners who had recently been on the road. In the dark, as we moved further and further away from each other, this disturbance was the only reminder left of the love of running that had bonded us together in the hotel lobby twelve hours ago. Otherwise we were on our own, the supporters' bus having already reached Sparta, where partners and children were now waiting.

At the 109-kilometre checkpoint I sat down to accept the offer of soup and tea, then rewarded myself with a change of socks and clean T-shirt before putting on my fluorescent jacket and strapping on my head torch. This was 9 kilometres further than I had ever previously run and amounted to 13 hours on the move without stopping. For the last hour I had run in the shadows, unnoticed, of two pale Finns, making me buoyant again at the thought that I was not alone, even though I had not exchanged a word with anyone since leaving Thierry 4 hours earlier.

To reach my night bag was the crossing of another psychological boundary. As I lit my head torch once the lights of the village were behind me, I became wholly a flame drawing a real strength from the burning furnace of the beam holding off the darkness, even if only by a few metres. Through the night the flashlights of those around me sparked like crashing photons. I kept my distance from the Finns, not wanting to startle them into trying to shake me off, so that when their lights disappeared around a corner I could see nothing but the haze of my own light in motion.

One thing became clear to me as I read the chaotic notes that I took in the days after the race, when my mind was still scarred. I knew at the time, even if I cannot fully believe it now, months later, that the pain was not going to be my undoing. I had left Corinth in better physical shape than I had been in Athens with all the nerves and junk of preparation finally flushed out. As I passed through the significant checkpoints at 90, 100, 109, 120 and 125 kilometres, although I was walking the slopes more than I had during the day, my legs still felt indestructibly powerful, and my feet had only mild abrasions. Those with previous experience of the Spartathlon concentrated on resisting the inevitable feeling of mental collapse by breaking the race down into its checkpoints, moving from each one to the next and not thinking beyond that. It had been Thierry's last piece of advice before I left him: that only by rationalising the process into digestible bites, rather than trying to take on the whole all at once, would I be able to compensate for my inner compass slowly but stubbornly pointing to home as the night took hold.

Every few hours I phoned Laurence to update her on my progress while I was signed in and out by the calm volunteers at the checkpoints, who offered tea and chocolate with patience and encouragement. As in Rotherham, these were the real heroes, staying up all night to make sure that we set off safely. They were a reminder that, whatever the outcome of this race, it was ultimately a selfish act, leaving the runners' loved ones to wait anxiously for the phone call announcing that it was all over.

Time passed more slowly now, gently doing its work. As we moved further into the darkness, I started to become troubled by a genuine fear that was crystallised by the knowledge that it would not get light until shortly after 7 a.m. I was set for the longest night of my life. Gilles had talked about this moment and had gripped my forearm, telling me that I must hold my nerve. To set foot into the night for the first time required a leap of faith – a blind stepping into the unknown. 'Now is the time to be brave,' he said, echoing the traditional phrase of the French executioner as he entered the condemned man's cell. I had to remember that I was not alone. We had all committed more than a year of training, all of our skill, strength and intelligence, maybe even our very existence, just to stay the course and keep ourselves alive. It was for this that I had spent those hours wrapped in bin liners and woolly hats in the middle of the summer, sweat gushing off me.

After the 120-kilometre checkpoint, the bouts of melancholy became more frequent. In real terms nothing had changed. The Finns were still 50 metres up ahead, while I was as rigidly disciplined as I had been all day in keeping my pace down, walking the slopes and listening to my body's demands for more food and water. But every runner will tell you of those moments of despondency, the inescapable desire to be somewhere else that, over time, starts to grip more stubbornly.

The challenge that we runners had set ourselves was in part to stand at the outer limits of our moral courage and see what we are capable of, while experiencing that heightened sense of moral being. The essence of running is a metaphor for life and to run the Spartathlon was a way for us to become better people. There was no one to stop me from quitting, and I was in part carrying on simply to see when the last step would come. What I had never seen before was the physical and emotional limits of my own capacities. For the first time in my life I was living at the absolute extremity of my own being, experiencing a frisson of danger in this discomfort zone. Despite the growing fatigue, it was electrifying.

In the year that it had taken me to get to Athens, running had become, melodramatically, my reason for living. It had become the way that I experienced the world, by running through it as well as by answering the question of how best to act. Each time I had come back from spending hours and hours on the road, I had the impression that there was so much that had been resolved and which now needed to be transformed into a story to convey my journey's epic quality. Saint-Exupéry understood well these moments of clarity: 'Once again I have rubbed shoulders with a truth without fully comprehending it,' he wrote. 'I thought I was lost forever, I thought I had reached the bottom of the pit of despair, and then with renunciation I knew peace. It seems that at such times we discover ourselves and become our own friends. Nothing can break down that sense of completeness, that fulfilment within us of some fundamental need unknown until that moment.' It was only out on the road, running for mile after mile, that I was able to work out what was required of me as a morally sentient being.

Every runner speaks of the surprise at how quickly bodily sensation can alter and the feeling of aching comfort transform itself into a pall of disconsolation. We had reached the foot of the mountains now and the sky was utterly dark, the moon weak, a dirty brown behind the clouds. Ahead of me the Finns turned off the main road back onto the mountain paths and we heard the promised thunderstorm cracking ahead of us. They too were suffering, I could see. Their legs reached down and forward with a slow pedalling movement, like a man descending through the trapdoor of a loft and feeling for a ladder with his feet. They were running with a clumsy arthritic tread; it was the gait of the dying, yet pathetically funny to watch. There was no longer any sign of the graceful, beautifully balanced rhythm that they had started with. It was a sclerotic, seizured movement that made an onlooker fearful that they might break at any moment. But they were still heroically pushing forward, and I had to stay with them.

By 10 p.m. I was meandering across the road, and my mind was starting to burn out. Words and fragments of sentences that had kept me occupied for the last few hours now vanished altogether, as the image fades when a television is switched off. However, it brought a new clarity – of a kind. Just as the psychologist R. S. Woodworth had observed, 'often we have to get away from speech to think more clearly'. Whatever linear progression of thought there had previously been had circled into a repetition 'You're going to take that 2 minutes and bank it.' Then I ceased to think at all and was left with a vast, intricate space in my brain.

When Cherry-Garrard was at the South Pole, he took with him Dickens' *Bleak House* and a volume of poetry that he found useful, 'because it gave one something to learn by heart and repeat during the blank hours of the daily march, when the idle mind is all too apt to think of food in times of hunger, or possibly of purely imaginary grievances'. Failure to follow this advice was my folly. Single words came stuttering out like a light bulb crackling to expire as a dense fog began to fill my head. With each step I seemed to be drowning further in warm, black milk.

On his decade-long journey home to Ithaca after the Trojan War, Odysseus was, according to Homer, told about the sirens, terrible creatures with birds' bodies and ugly women's heads, who sang so beautifully that all the passing sailors would jump in the sea to reach them, either drowning in the attempt or wrecking their ships on the rocks. On Circe's advice, Odysseus had his men tie him to the mast while they plugged their own ears with wax, so that he might hear the sirens' song without being able to jump. Crazed with longing by their music, Odysseus tried to signal to the crew to let him go, but they could hear nothing. It was their call that I was starting to hear. 'Enough. Come home,' the voices whispered. Over and over again.

I began to subject myself to emotional blackmail. 'Give me one reason to stop. Just one, and I will.' That was the test to ignore. 'Don't give in,' I tried to say to myself as I passed each checkpoint, but the goading voice gradually took hold of me in that last hour. 'Come home', it continued to whisper and there was no one to help me block it out.

It was around this time that I started to hallucinate. The moon had disappeared, leaving only the light from our head torches to help us pick out silhouettes against the rocks. Andy McMenemy, whom I had run with in Rotherham and who had run the Spartathlon the year before, talked of seeing seals flapping past him that were so real that he would step aside to let them pass. When they stopped with him he would shine his torch in their direction, only for them to immediately disappear. When Charles Lindbergh flew solo non-stop across the Atlantic, he heard voices as his mind began to wander. 'First one and then another presses forward to my shoulder to speak above the engine's voice . . . [or they] come out of the air itself, clear yet far away, travelling through distances that can't be measured by the scale of human miles . . . conversing and advising me on my flight, discussing problems of my navigation, reassuring me, giving me messages of importance unattainable in ordinary life.' What I needed, I realise now, was someone to talk to, some noise to fill my head. The unhinging process that had started in the summer out on the Thames was upon me again, and I could feel part of my mind falling away from me like the slow descent of the side of a house under a wrecker's ball.

Checkpoint 36 marked exactly halfway between Athens and Sparta. I arrived at 11 p.m. nearly 40 minutes ahead of the closing time, and sat down in the crowd of runners and supporters who were cooking meals on gas stoves or peering at graphs on laptops. A few runners, whom I had not seen since the morning, huddled under blankets. I was handed a bowl of pasta and ate it with a knife picked up from the floor before checking in with Laurence. The Finns were sitting quietly out of the way, massaging their calves and saying little. Five minutes later I was up and out of the checkpoint, thinking that they had already left. The road itself was indistinguishable but the lonely traces of head torches indicated a path that wound up towards a peak that was just visible in the moonlight. I was relieved. There was no way I was going to run that, so I zipped up my top and started to speed-march in search of the Finns.

Half an hour after leaving behind the empty pasta bowl, I started to question how much further I could actually go. It was 11.30 p.m. and the mountains were now starting to become an issue. I also knew that there were still 8 hours of darkness to wade through. As the minutes and then the hours accumulated, the more frequently I looked at my watch, the more I could feel each second form its own character before lurching on to the next. It was not just that I was slowing down; time itself seemed to have expanded, opening itself up to scrutiny at the atomic level.

The Finns were nowhere to be seen, and I realised too late that I had set off ahead of them. Running past the bus that would carry those with DNF (did not finish) added to their name only made it worse. I was sinking deeper into the warm milk. I could just stop. Here. And step onto the bus. An invisible force was crushing me. I could feel its weight, its hypnotic powers; it was forcing me to think how it wanted, feel how it dictated. Wherever this force had come from, it was now inside me: it could dissolve my will and cause my heart to stop beating.

Only people who have never felt such a force themselves can be surprised at how quickly others submit to it. Those who have felt it, on the other hand, express astonishment that a man can rebel against it even for a moment – with one sudden cry of anger, the drive to reach one more checkpoint, one small gesture of defiant motion.

Faced with real suffering for the first time in my life, I speculated momentarily on my chances of going to heaven. But even as I thought it, I knew this was another trick of my disintegrating mind. After all, I could just stop; it was not as though I was stuck on a frozen plateau miles from safety or stranded on an exposed peak, although my isolation and peril felt real enough. I did not care in any case – I could not have wept if I had tried. I had no wish to review the mistakes of my past, but my past did seem to have been a bit wasted. There was no greater end than that which this journey was satisfying, although there were plenty of other things I could have spent the last twelve months doing that would have been infinitely more pleasurable.

But then I had read Saint-Exupéry's beautiful memoir of his time as a courier pilot, *Wind, Sand and Stars*. There he wrote lovingly about these very moments of being aloft, when one suddenly 'passes beyond the borders of the real world' and into a realm so elemental that it seems other-worldly. As we rose in altitude and became mired in the fog of fatigue, I felt, however fleetingly, that I had become elevated 'above the trivialities of life into a new understanding'. Athens was a distant continent and I had traversed something metaphysical, not just geographical. I was being taken 'out of knowledge', as the poet John Clare described it, moving away from the familiar to a new perspective that is not purely the product of exhaustion and hallucination but which comes through a natural transformation of the body and mind in unknown territories.

In his *Notebooks*, Samuel Coleridge instructed those who take to the mountains to prepare to be confronted with the collision of a hugely developed sense of inner and outer reality, with neither sense giving ground. Perhaps this was true for those who had fortified themselves sufficiently, but on those mountain roads of dust and rubble I felt a final severance from articulated life – a profound sense of both disorientation and being forgotten. No cars came up this way, and up ahead the air was rent by lightning. Patches of grey flashed between mountain tops.

There was an irony that, at the very moment I was

falling apart, the friends against whom I had not been able to compete at school – and to whom at the beginning of this adventure I had in some way wanted to prove something – were all gathered together for the first time in twelve years to celebrate an imminent wedding. If only they could see me now, I might have thought, but I was too tormented with fatigue to care much in any case.

The road seemed never to stop going up. I couldn't believe this to be true since it bore no relation to the graph of the changing altitude of the course that I had pinned to the wall at home. What this graph showed was that mathematics had only a superficial relationship to the outside world, and when addressed like this it had no correlation to humankind. There was nothing here except for the crunch of mountain gravel and, underneath, the curved shape of the earth. Everything around me was as dead as it had been 2,500 years ago when Pheidippides had run this very course to save Western civilisation. The fundamentals of our nature, the laws of our moral behaviour, all stem from this blighted terrain of jagged rocks and cliff faces. The morality of the Bible, of mankind itself, had been written out on roads like this.

The long, lone ridge opened across the skyline like the low hull of a submarine. Through the solitude I was no longer forcing myself from within, but was being lured through that horizon and on to others. They disappeared from view and from memory. There was no moon now, only black asphalt that extended to the stars, with the next checkpoint another 4 inconsolable miles away. The spirit of the Peloponnese was breathing over us, spreading a mother's shawl beneath our exhausted feet. I had the feeling that I was capsizing, my inner ear disorientated from motion sickness, and I was sure that I was about to keel over at any moment, having split apart from head to navel.

After 17 hours, it all corroded in an instant. I could not breathe, could not move, was too weak to talk or to think, or even to be dismayed as a cherished fantasy dissolved. Glued to the road, in the space of 10 kilometres I had turned from indestructible to an invalid. I stared ahead momentarily into the dark, trying to imagine the finish line, something I knew I should never do. My head felt impossibly heavy and rolled onto my chest.

The place where I collapsed was like the scenery from the Middle Ages. I would like to think that, with poetic intuition, I understood that in the darkness as midnight chimed, it was the end of a dream, that there was a neat closure in not being able to run on into the next day. But all I could think about was how relieved I was that I didn't have to run any further.

The table at Checkpoint 38 was set up by the side of the path at the entrance to a small chapel. I sat down on a plastic chair facing a bush and tried to think what

I was going to do. As I did so, I felt part of my brain rushing forward and my stomach crashing upwards. No one was surprised to see me throwing up. Out of inexperience, I had been taking on large amounts of water, even though the temperature had dropped dramatically, and all the careful preparations I had made were negated in an instant.

I had 40 minutes until the checkpoint closed. Almost immediately after I had been sick, my body started to shut down. I knew from Mark Cockbain that this would happen. I still had plenty of time to collect myself, but my eyes were closing and I began to shiver. 'You won't feel any worse,' he had promised. 'Just remind yourself of that.'

I felt drunk, elated but uncoordinated, entranced and incoherent. It was like the rapture of the deep – *l'ivresse des grandes profondeurs* – as the diving pioneer Jacques-Yves Cousteau called it. 'I like it,' he wrote, 'and fear it like doom. It destroys the instinct for life.' My mind had become disorientated, the hallucinations combining with conscious thought to fixate on delusional ideas, and the voices of those near by reached me as cries heard while dreaming. I tried to stand up but my legs gave way beneath me.

'Enough.' I gestured pathetically to the race organiser. 'I'm finished.' But it came out as a breath of air too weak to be heard the first time. 'Excuse me. I've stopped.'

Everything changed suddenly. They asked me twice

if I really was going to quit and I was told I needed to hand in my numbers. And please sign here.

'We'll take you to the bus.'

'Thank you,' I mumbled.

The Finns arrived as the Land Rover appeared, kicking up dust, and they politely asked for a cup of tea. Hunched over the long stilts of their legs, they stood motionless, feigning death, their faces pale in the light of the oil lamp, macabre and sorrowing, like those of drowned men. I knew that this was how I looked too. 'The deepest objective experiences are also the most universal, because through them one reaches the original source of life,' the melancholy Romanian philosopher, E. M. Cioran, had written. There was no other way to put it: to suffer was to witness a universal knowledge, a metaphysical revelation. Whatever pain others might feel, I was feeling it right now. I only realised much later that something within me had broken at that moment, and that my will, the universal will, had been exposed to a divine knowledge.

The Finns, however, were not finished yet, since they had not made the mistake of going off too quickly at the last checkpoint, and soon they were on their way.

The bus was full of the dead and the dying, slumped across every seat revealing the sub-soil of human nature. Legs were curled up, covered in dust, salt, vomit and blood. The bandages and the popping veins would have taken hold of anyone's imagination, prompting a flood of empathy, but unless you have been there you cannot know how profoundly humbling it is to feel that you have been thrown up by the sea, battered, limp and life-less. There was no violence in the exhaustion that is felt over shorter distances, even marathons. Beneath the bare and glaring lights, all the runners who had quit before me lay asleep as though dead drunk. Some of them I had not seen since the start line. Others had passed me by silently hours before. By the time I finished, after 17 hours and 85 miles, 180 others had quit.

During the day I had heard that people had quit for dramatic reasons. One runner was insisting that he would carry on, only to be forcefully returned to his seat, told that he was in shock and would be put in the back of an ambulance. There was one cracked skull and multiple cases of dehydration. Very few dropped out between here and Sparta, suggesting that, theoretically, I had got over the worst of it and that, if I had carried on, statis-tically I would have stood a high chance of being one of the 130 who finished on time. But I had learnt the hard way to be honest with myself. I could not have run any further. I gathered my belongings and crum-pled against the window as the exhaustion entered me through my closing eyes.

We arrived at the hotel in Sparta at 3 a.m. Ahead of me James, another first-timer from London whom I had last seen an hour out of Corinth, stepped off the bus like a sleepwalker, looking straight ahead, numb and enraptured, his eyes open but unfocused. Laurence found me in reception. An Italian was trying to get me to drink some flat Coke, as we sat around waiting to be told what to do. Ushering me quietly into our bedroom, she tried to get me to open my mouth wide enough to eat some bread and jam, but could get only a corner in. I chewed it until my mouth was dry before swallowing. Following her biblical instructions: *take*, *eat*, she helped me through the basic mechanics of undressing and getting into bed as Friday, 24 September 2009 was finally snuffed out.

I woke up through the night to hear a staccato rain bouncing off the roof. My legs were twitching, overheating and burning up. I sipped water, my throat still tight, while my stomach ached. I was still woozy with the disorientation of dehydration, and continued to drift in and out of a troubled sleep.

The church bells rang at five o'clock to signal the first runner home, the Japanese favourite. Two hours later I got up, thinking about the Finns who would still be out there somewhere, crawling off the mountain like insects down the side of a glass. Stop. Feel. Stop. Feel. I stood for as long as I could bear under the shower, shrivelled and shrunken as an old man, and then returned to bed. The white bed sheets flowed like a balm over my body, but it could not cure me as I continued to twist and turn, trying in vain to get my body to settle into sleep.

For the first day I did not know what I wanted or what I wanted to do. My stomach both ached for food and in rejection of it. The soles of my feet felt as though they had been scorched and were horribly tender. Great flanks of skin had turned bloody, deep beneath the surface, and for two days my feet were too swollen for shoes. When I finally did emerge to shuffle along the lunch queue, I ate the first of five full meals, including four portions of chips, four pork chops, two hamburgers, a steak and a bowl of pasta.

Sparta is a one-street town. After lunch Laurence propped me up as I crept with miniature steps to the statue of King Leonidas, whose feet the competitors must kiss to signal the end of their race. For the rest of the afternoon we sat at the finish line, clapping home the pale, exhausted runners in the grey light, flanked by excited children on bicycles cheering them on.

As the afternoon progressed, more runners who had been pulled from the course emerged from the hotel, and there was only one subject that we could talk about. The excited chatter of Athens was replaced by excuses or explanations as to why we had not finished. In truth, we all knew that those of us who had not completed the race had simply not prepared well enough. H. G. Wells wrote that 'the forceps of our minds are clumsy things, and crush the truth a little in the course of taking hold of it'. As the 36–hour time limit approached and I started to spot those I had run with, the half-formed illusion that I could have continued rapidly evaporated. Involuntarily I cast my mind back to Checkpoint 38 and wished that I could have carried on. Laurence could see what I was doing.

'You couldn't have gone any further. You didn't see the state you were in when you arrived back at the hotel. Be happy with what you achieved. You couldn't have run another mile.'

I knew that she was right. These runners had trained for years for this race. It had taken me twelve months to be able to cover those 85 miles. The one person I met who finished the Spartathlon on his first attempt had been running ultra–distances for ten years, but he said it was 'pour la dernière fois'. He would never come back.

On the Saturday night the town square in Sparta was transformed with advertising hoardings and plastic chairs. There would be light shows, dancing and fireworks to honour the top three male and female runners. There is little reason for tourists to come to Sparta and the mayor knew that he had just one opportunity to cele-brate its existence with the outside world. Up on stage limped the three fastest men, the Japanese favourite, a Dane and a Norwegian, followed by the women. As he had won the race in 23:48, it was announced that the winner would sing his own national anthem solo to the crowd of 3,000, which he did unhesitatingly before bowing slightly to the delighted audience.

On the Sunday morning we returned to Athens. I saw Mark Cockbain for the first time since the morning of the race.

'How did it go?' I asked, not knowing what phraseology to use.

'I finished, so it was a good race.'

For the week that followed, it was only when I was suspended in water that I could not feel my legs burn. My feet wept for days. Blisters, forming and popping under the nails, turned the skin a mottled black as the damage done to the tissues slowly revealed itself like some peculiar deep-sea creature. The swelling did not fully subside for a fortnight.

I never did see the two Finns again, and when I retraced my steps, trying to remember every detail of the place where I had collapsed, it was to them that my imagination turned, wondering whether they – and by extension I – could have finished if I had tried for one last checkpoint.

~~Never Again~~

If only this was a work of fiction.

Having brought you this far and with so few pages left, I should at least be able to offer some kind of resolution. If this were a novel, it would now be time to bring neatly together all the narrative lines, leaving you content that the circle has been completed. You could then close the book with a sigh of satisfaction. For a month or so I believed it might be possible.

As I lay in the hotel room in Sparta, the thought came to me: 'A week ago I was not born.' A week ago I had not yet experienced an intensity of being that pierced me as an arrow thuds into a tree. The Spartathlon had given me a glimpse of a universal truth. I had been smelted into a different ore. I had seen, as though for the first time, a kingdom of earth and iron, blood and flesh. All of us had been reduced to an arrangement of sweat, blood and vomit by the dirt and the brutality of the landscape. I knew now how a man might be split apart.

How can I describe the deep, vibrant pleasure I felt in those weeks afterwards? Perhaps it was a little like the moment just before a child bursts into tears. He knows that he is going to cry and he does nothing about it. He has no shame, he wants to drown in it, to be swallowed up by his emotions. As the fatigue receded, I was less able to hold on to the precise memory exactly what I had been through. The warm, numbing calm stayed with me longer, and yet, in time, that went too. I found that the saddest of all, since I had hoped, too optimistically, that once I had achieved that state of self-obliteration, it would remain with me permanently, lifting me above the grubby banalities of everyday life.

I have always been proud of my ability to subordinate my life to logic, and marathon running is seldom as bad as we imagine. A great fuss is rightly made of those who do it for the first and the only time, because it may be the hardest physical challenge that they ever put themselves through. But we all know the truth that really anyone can run a marathon, given enough time.

This race, by contrast, beggared any language: no words could really completely express its horror because it did not just simply represent, but *was*, a Dostoevskian exchange of physical well-being for peace of mind. Here, as in no other race, the broken runner begs to be pulled from the course, just as a sick or wounded animal offers itself up to be killed.

When Carl Jung was shown a photograph of Augustine Courtauld, who had exiled himself for the six months of winter in the Arctic in the 1930s, he saw the face of a man 'stripped of his *persona*, his public self stolen, leaving his true self naked before the world'. To think back to the precise moment when my own race was over was to see something similar in myself.

This was not what John Foden had set out to do twenty-five years previously. He just wanted to see whether it could be done. Nevertheless, the Spartathlon runners bring to the road everything that they are whilst being cruelly exposed to the elements. That is the price we pay for this kind of adventure. Some recover easily and move on to the next challenge, but for others there is an overdraft on their mental and physical capacity that can never quite be paid off.

As there are far greater runners than me, so there are far more articulate writers who have encapsulated the fundamental characteristics that draw individuals to their particular obsessions. Although the year I spent in preparation for the Spartathlon was never an academic exercise, since it was too physically and mentally destructive not to leave emotional scars, I had not thought that I would be drawn into a compulsion to put it before everything else in my life. Previously, I liked to proudly say that I was a marathoner and I would wait for that moment's silence while people sized me up. Now there ceased to be any distinction between my ordinary life and my life as a runner. I lived to run. It needed no further explanation.

For a moment, I had really thought that the transformation I had undergone would extend to the world around me, that things could not carry on the way that they had. When Cherry-Garrard came back from the Antarctic after a harrowing eighteen-month expedition, he knew that nothing essential had changed. Even in the trenches of the First World War, he was forever being hassled to recount his journey by people who did not understand what he and his team had been through. How could they? Cherry himself admitted that he barely understood it.

For three months I slept for 14 hours a day. My body gradually healed, the swelling in my feet subsided, the blisters burst and blackened, and after Christmas my legs eventually lost their dumb ache. I had known beforehand – because I could see it in the eyes of those who came back year after year and still had not finished the race – that to quit before getting to Sparta meant to be left suspended, eternally perhaps, between two points, able to go neither forward nor back. However, in those first months, I was convinced that, even though I had failed, I had satisfied the contradictory and conflicting motives that had compelled me to attempt to run from Athens to Sparta in the first place. I thought I could get on with the rest of my life. With that conviction came a real sense that I was finally at peace with myself, that I could calmly return to my sedentary existence a wiser, better person – for ever. And this is what I wish I could offer you – a single reason why everyone should attempt this race just once. Yet, this is not a work of fiction, and I can do little more than tell you what happened next.

Soon enough, the silt of everyday life returned – the soft and sticky slowing-down of both motion and thought. These were the first signs that I was starting to lose my grip on the knowledge, the state of grace, that I had found on the road to Sparta. I became impatient, restless and boorish. I could feel the film of grime returning to my skin, which was not surprising since I was not running, sweating or showering nearly as much as I had done for the previous year. This was how I had perceived the world before the race, and I did not like what I saw. I put on weight, I started to drink again. In my inebriation I remembered the distance I had placed between myself and other people by running all those miles up the Thames. And in the hangovers that I got out of bed with, twice, three, sometimes four times a week, I felt the same deadening exhaustion in my body that I had had when I awoke the morning after running 40 miles. As time drew me further away from the mountain top in Greece, I began to feel as though I had to wade through the day just to keep up.

While, in part, this was my old self returning, my

unhappiness also came from knowing that I had left something of myself up at Checkpoint 38. There was a better person, an idealised version of the man I wanted to be, who had never returned. That person and that place quickly became something to dream about.

It was not long before the lust to return to Greece started to gnaw away at me. It came most strongly during the night, perhaps most obviously because my body was still recovering, and violent twitches in my sleep would wake me. I had promised Laurence that I would never go back, and it troubled me deeply to wonder how long I could maintain that fiction. 'At what point am I going to stop?' George Mallory asked his friend Geoffrey Winthrop Young. I am humble enough not to compare my obsession with the desire that led Mallory to his death, but the possessive nature of what we both did was there, nonetheless – almost mocking me from outside that chapel: unfinished business that had to be attended to.

Comfort came in the knowledge that others were thinking the same too. Gilles had told me that he had started planning his second attempt within days of returning to France. Once we had scattered back to our corners of the world, I liked to imagine the other runners waking in the dark, as winter encroached, thinking about how they would finish the race next time. And the tragedy was that we all knew that, until we had dealt with that unfinished business, we could never be fully satisfied. It was as if we had been shown a glimpse of a route to eternal contemplation, but had been told – 'Not yet!'

Back in the office, I found a 1,000-word email from Gilles with a strategy written out in precise detail that would get me to the finish line. It had taken him ten years of running the Spartathlon to work out what the year's training should be like, and how to get through the heat, the night and the mountains at every stage of the race itself. Even having finished it again this year, he wrote that his plan still needed modifying. For the year leading up to the Spartathlon, he competed in every 24-hour and 48-hour race he could find. It was only by doing this that he knew that he could prepare himself mentally for getting over the mountains in the dark and staying in one piece.

Similarly, for the final weeks of preparation, as he put in 2 hours at lunchtime every day, he would eat very little, and then only what he would be offered at the race checkpoints, to prevent his stomach from reacting violently to the change of diet. For six months prior to the Spartathlon he would sleep no more than 6 hours a night, preferably less: possibly the most challenging part of the strategy, since when you have run 100 miles sleeping is all you want to do.

When it came to the race itself, Gilles's regime followed common sense. He ate a little every hour, so as to not overload his stomach, preferring soup and energy bars to anything more substantial. He drank small amounts of water during the day, and then tea and coffee through the night stages to keep him awake and warm.

Psychologically, he divides the race into three equal parts, concentrating on nothing further than the next checkpoint as he looks first to Corinth (where Thierry had abandoned the race), the 195-kilometre check-point, high into the second mountain range, which he breaks up with speedwalking the ascents. The final section takes him to Sparta itself, where even on his twelfth attempt he had to take a deep breath and have faith in himself to finish, so exhausted was he by this stage.

Gilles has been running ultra-distance races all year round for over ten years, but the Spartathlon is the pinnacle of his racing calendar. From the way he spoke of it with such reverence, it was clear to me that to take part was the culmination of a life's work, and every other race that he ran was simply a way of preparing himself for another attempt. There is no way to get through the heat or the night without enduring the hard miles and, as I was quick to realise, even this does not guarantee success. In the end, success, as measured by people like Gilles and Mark Cockbain, is down to getting across the finish line in under 36 hours, and that can be done only with practice and patience. Even they had failed to finish on their first attempt. If their advice can be reduced to a soundbite, it might be that, in the same way that Malcolm Gladwell argues that it takes 10,000 hours of practice to excel in any discipline, so it takes 10,000 miles to complete the Spartathlon.

As I read Gilles's email, in an instant I could feel my body returning to that dusty track, thighs quivering, head slightly bowed, as I moved to the rhythm of the mountain road. Surrounded by the paperwork of another office day, I was grateful to be cast back so suddenly to a half-dead land that I had left behind in the middle of the night. As I stared out of the office window as the rain set in, each line of that email represented a manifestation of the secret desire that anyone who has pined for adventure will have shared.

The Spartathlon is one of the few doors the modern world has left open on risk. Or as Lionel Terray wrote, it is 'one of the ways out of the armour-plating humdrumness in which civilisation imprisons us, and for which we are not very well adapted'. We so rarely feel a cold, sweating fear for our lives, whether real or imaginary.

I wonder whether we would be less fractious and kinder if we experienced more fear, if we took ourselves more frequently to the edge of this precipice and stared over it. Although mountains are beautiful and Arctic landscapes dramatic, there really is no need for them. Just close the front door behind you and be off in any direction, since all you need is your two feet and the open road. The beauty of motion, the ecstasy of freedom from a hurried, over-sophisticated world, requiring little financial cost and limited innate skill: this is the privilege of the running experience.

At the age of eighty-nine, Bertrand Russell wrote: 'I must, before I die, find some means of saying the essential thing which is in me, which I have not yet said, a thing which is neither love nor hate nor pity nor scorn but the very breath of life, shining and coming from afar, which will link into human life the immensity, the frightening, wondrous and implacable forces of the non-human.'

He knew, of course, that he had not done it yet because it could not be done. What mattered, above all else, was the act itself. Philippe Petit knew it too. While he was preparing to walk across the wire between the Twin Towers, a friend brought along a cine-camera to document the event for posterity, as well as financial gain. Petit saw through it immediately: 'Either we do a bank robbery, or we do a film about a bank robbery. We cannot do both.' The act itself was pure, a chance to do something extraordinary.

What I learnt in the months that followed was that when I returned to the Spartathlon, as I knew I would, I would have to do it not to tell a story about a journey into adulthood, or to excavate the reasons why we run. I would have to take it on, silently, simply for the sake of running itself.

★

My modest hope is that these pages will point you in the right direction to uncover your own reasons for why you run. It is deeply personal, of course, but we can also learn from those who have been there before us. Through the process of identifying the many elements that make up the inclinations of the runner, I wanted to show that there is a story that unites us all – the elite, the ultra-distance runner and those who stick stubbornly to their 5 miles and no more on a Sunday morning. I suppose that, in this process, I had hoped that a coherent recon-ciliation would emerge of why we do this, day after day, week after week. By starting with the familiar and digging towards a primary bedrock of a universal explanation, one that we all *know* is in our hearts but may not have articulated well enough for others to understand, I hoped to give some kind of answer to the question: why do we do this? As you might have guessed, there is no neat answer. There is no point at which we stop. We just keep returning, giving ourselves over to these huge distances, because this is what we do.

Almost two years to the day after Jean-Louis died, our son was born. In the course of Laurence's pregnancy the signs of suffering finally lifted from Marie-Jo's expres-sion. Her anxiety about the future was gradually replaced by a warmth of love and hope, and the person she had been before re-emerged in its entirety. Some days are better than others, but most of the time it is difficult now to believe that any of the last two years ever happened. At times, however, even though we had learnt to be patient and above all learnt to listen, we had asked too much of her.

In the same way, I asked too much of running when I thought that one race would transform me, just like that, for ever. There is no ascetic state in which we can remain for all time, forever transcended out of our everyday lives. There is only the possibility of another attempt at the race.

My father told me long ago that to become better people we needed to rid ourselves of all vanities. I had nodded when he said this, but I didn't understand at all what he meant. Now I think I do. Running is not about fitness, competition, or even other people. It is simply about becoming a more sentient person, living what the novelist Alice Munro called a more authentic life.

Postscript:

The Empty City
Field Notes from a Runner's Paradise

For the first year of my son's life I hardly ran at all. Amid the chaos of the early months of fatherhood, the furthest I ran was the double London Marathon from Big Ben to the start and back, and I was piled so high with caffeine, since he had not slept for two nights, that when it was over I could barely remember having done it at all.

The reasons were both banal and familiar. I had reached adulthood and every mile had to be stolen against the clock, and when I did go out I would, invariably, cut short the run in case something had happened in my absence. Family life became a tightly choreographed routine – each run was precursored with days of planning: when will you leave? When will you be back? Should we wait for lunch? Places I had come to know intimately with my feet, whose every elevation, texture and contour I could have once recited, were locked away in the attic with the winter running clothes.

To neuter the fear that my running days were over I

bought new running shoes and, improbably, I joined the Serpentine Running Club. On Wednesdays after work I would, too rarely, join them by Speakers' Corner in Hyde Park to cover seven miles before heading to the pub. I began to realise how much my centre of gravity had shifted. My balance was off because of the weight that I had put on in the past year, and after an hour I could feel my legs disappearing off at peculiar angles as they tired. I had known, if only fleetingly, what it was like to run with grace. This was not it.

But could some form of that previous life still be captured, however fleetingly? At night I would creep, barefoot, onto the roof of our house while the family were asleep and sit looking out east to the City and the horizon towards St Paul's and the North Downs, and imagine being out there on the pavements reeling in some mythical finish line. And it was here that I kept the dream of returning to Greece alive.

In the beginning I returned to the maps. They showed London's postal districts packed out like squares of wheat. With the glimpse of the skyline in front of me I had the second great aesthetic revelation of my life. The maps were sublime. I had never contemplated an object as magnificent, as rich in emotion and meaning as this 1/25,000 representation of the capital. Each borough, every side street, was fully represented down to the direction from which they should be approached. I felt the thrill of human life, of millions of souls, most who would be asleep as I nudged my finger over them, unseen. This was 'the other place' that the novelist Haruki Murakami talked of disappearing to. Some nights I would stare at them too long and I would reconcile that the maps were far more interesting than the territory, that I could stay here and live out the adventure simply by tracing my fingers over the contours.

Apart from during races I had never run late into the night and I was tentative when it came to closing the door behind me. It is no coincidence that I started running further and harder the more settled into our new family life we all became, when my teeth no longer felt like they were going to fall out of my head from all the sugar that I was consuming just to stay awake. Over the months, night running became a counter-point to my new daily routine. I ran for hours East and North, past five storeys of empty car parks, echoing the silence of miles of uninhabited streets and dark, locked offices, into suburbs I had grown to know intimately in two-dimension. Towards dawn I would look up and find myself, as if by accident, miles from home. Next came a shift in the city's distant commotion – the day's begin-ning. I had to get off the streets. In the dark I had seen something of the runner I had once been, breath hovering out in front of me, my legs vanished completely from view as, once again, I became the single eye in motion.

What surprised me most was to see just how many people there were on the streets – running at 4am. If we acknowledged each other, it was only briefly, as is always the case. Even though it is a growing phenomenon, each of us is locked into our own reverie. We come here to get away from other people, to enjoy these precious moments of solitude before normal daylight service resumes.

Making for home down Primrose Hill and round Regent's Park, I would scale the perimeter of Hyde Park, the runner as transgressor, finally liberated. I would turn off my head torch and switch from my fluorescent top to a black disguise to run undetected as the first planes sparkled in along the Heathrow flight path. Out the other side I would wait for the traffic and when the moment came, fling each leg over the fence, scared for the first time in a long while at the thought of being caught. Through Vauxhall, Portuguese and Somali families would already be rising to get shutters up and fruit arranged on the pavement stalls. Leaves and litter spewed across the road, apocalyptically. I had reached the end of the world. Back behind the front door I would shower, change and crawl onto the roof to watch the city wake, waiting for the first yelp of the morning to indicate that the day had begun and that the adventure was over for another night.

Acknowledgements

Everyone is in debt, and I am no different.

My first thanks must go to the people who have helped me write this book. Rory Coleman accepted the challenge of getting me fit for the Spartathlon and chiselled out of a lump of flesh an athlete I never thought I was capable of being. Eleanor Birne helped me to carve out a proper narrative after my return from the Spartathlon, for which I am hugely grateful. My thanks go to Clive Priddle at PublicAffairs, who understands well what these distances mean to us. Also to Laetitia Rutherford, who first saw the seed of an idea and set me off on this journey, as well as to all the teams at John Murray, especially Victoria Murray-Browne, Lyndsey Ng, Nikki Barrow, Jason Bartholomew, James Spackman, Lucy Hale and Polly Ho-Yen, who made me feel like one of the family and Celia Levett, who copy-edited the manuscript beautifully. A special mention should also be made of Jonny Butler, who gave me invaluable advice during the genesis of the book.

The ultra-distance running world was one that I had known of only vaguely when I set out to write this story, but I was welcomed with open arms by all those I met, and it is their contributions that have provided the real richness to this book. Particular thanks go to John Foden, Andy McMenemy, Mark Cockbain, Nitish Zuidema, Thierry and Gilles, and the two unnamed Finns whom I followed through most of the night out of Corinth, as well as all those who gave me priceless advice in my preparations. Thank you also to the volunteers who made possible the races I ran. The weather during the Round Rotherham 50-mile Ultra that I took part in was so bad that the date has since been moved. If you were one of the brave people who stood in the cold and the rain, handing out home-made sandwiches and jelly beans – thank you. I don't think I would have made it without your help.

The year I got married, I suggested to my close friends that we run the Paris Marathon for my stag party. Alex Orme was the only person to accept. Many of the miles I spent running along the Thames on Sunday mornings were in his company, for which I am eternally in his debt. However, it was when he agreed to run the course of the 2009 London Marathon with me under the cover of night, and then came and coaxed me around forty-four laps of a forest in the Amsterdam 100-kilometre Ultra to qualify for the Spartathlon – neither of which I describe in great detail here – that

I realised what true friendship is. Thank you also to Iain Chapple, who took me with him on a first attempt at the Bob Graham Round, and who probably put the idea of the Spartathlon in my head in the first place when he came back from the Marathon des Sables only to promptly check into hospital. Thanks also to all those I work with who have had to put up with a year of me walking through the office in my running kit twice a day every day.

I started writing this book to answer a simple question: why do we run? In the course of writing it and training, my life underwent a seismic shift of tectonic magnitude that turned it into a journey into adulthood, thereby forcing me to go back and look at where my own story had begun. I could not have done this, of course, without my parents who gave me the eyes to see the world and the feet to run across it – thank you. And to my brother Matthew, whose story this is, in part, too. My deepest thanks as well to my mother-in-law Marie-Jo and my brother-in-law Pierre for letting me tell their story too. Thank you also to Henrik Becker-Christensen, Inge and Halle, and Regitze Hess for navigating me through the muddy waters of my family history.

Anyone who runs knows that it is a lonely business, but we would do well to remember that it is lonely too for those we leave behind when we set off on our adventures. Waking up to an empty bed is no way to start the day. Laurence, it is an impossible task to thank you enough for your understanding in letting me embark on this odyssey. Whether it was putting up with the anxiety of every hour that I spent running ultra-distance races, picking up the pieces of my body when I did eventually return, or taking a thick red pen to the early drafts of the manuscript, I quite simply could not have done this without you. That this process took place in a year of such personal tragedy makes the selfless blessing you gave me more saintly still: *without you, no book.*

Further Reading

Ackroyd, Peter, *Thames: Sacred River*, Chatto & Windus, 2007

Allen, Benedict, *The Faber Book of Exploration*, Faber & Faber, 2004

Allison, Don, *Running Through the Wall: Personal Encounters with the Ultramarathon*, Breakaway Books, 2003

Askwith, Richard, *Feet in the Clouds: A Story of Fell Running and Obsession*, Arum Press Ltd, 2005

Austin, Michael W., *Running and Philosophy: A Marathon for the Mind*, Wiley-Blackwell, 2007

Bach, Steven, *Leni: The Life and Work of Leni Riefenstahl*, Abacus, 2008

Baker, J. A., *The Peregrine*, NYRB Classics, 2005

Bakewell, Sarah, *How to Live: A Life of Montaigne in One Question and Twenty Attempts at an Answer*, Chatto & Windus, 2010

Bannister, Sir Roger, *The Four Minute Mile*, Lyons Press, 2004

Bascomb, Neal, *The Perfect Mile: The Race to Break the Four Minute Mile*, Willow, 2005

Boetius, *The Consolation of Philosophy*, Oxford Paperbacks, 2008

Brant, John, *Duel in the Sun: Alberto Salazar, Dick Beardsley, and America's Greatest Marathon*, Rodale Press, 2007

Bruce, C. G., *The Assault on Mount Everest 1922*, Pilgrims Publishing, 2004

Bryant, John, *The London Marathon*, Arrow Books Ltd, 2006

Burke, Edmund, *A Philosophical Enquiry into the Origin of Our Ideas of the Sublime and Beautiful*, Oxford Paperbacks, 2008

Cherry-Garrard, Apsley, *The Worst Journey in the World*, Vintage, 2010

Cioran, E. M., *The Trouble with Being Born*, Little, Brown and Company, 2009

Clare, Horatio, *A Single Swallow: Following an Epic Journey from South Africa to South Wales*, Vintage, 2010

Cocker, Mark, *Crow Country*, Vintage, 2008

Coleridge, Samuel Taylor, *Coleridge: Among the Lakes and Mountains: From his Notebooks, Letters and Poems*, Folio Society, 1991

Conrad, Joseph, *The Mirror of the Sea*, BiblioBazaar, 2007

Cousteau, Jacques-Yves, *The Silent World*, National Geographic Books, 2004

Crane, David, *Scott of the Antarctic: A Life of Courage and Tragedy in the Extreme South*, Harper Perennial, 2006

Deakin, Roger, *Waterlog: A Swimmer's Journey Through Britain*, Vintage, 2000

Denison, Jim, *The Greatest: The Haile Gebrselassie Story*, Breakaway Books, 2004

Eliot, T. S., *The Waste Land and Other Poems*, Faber & Faber, 2002

Fiennes, William, *The Snow Geese*, Picador, 2010

Fixx, James F., *The Complete Book of Running*, Penguin, 1991

Gooley, Tristan, *The Natural Navigator*, Virgin Books, 2010

Griffiths, Jay, *Wild: An Elemental Journey*, Penguin, 2008

Hamilton, James, *Turner: A Life*, Sceptre, 1998

Heinrich, Bernd, *Why We Run: A Natural History*, Harper, 2002

Herbert, A. P., *The Thames*, Weidenfeld & Nicolson, 1966

Herodotus, *The Histories*, Penguin, 2003

Herzog, Maurice, *Annapurna: The First Conquest of an 8000-metre Peak*, Pimlico, 1997

Hill, David, *Turner on the Thames*, Yale University Press, 1993

Hoare, Philip, *Leviathan, or the Whale*, Fourth Estate, 2009

Huntford, Roland, *Nansen*, Abacus, 2001

James, William, *The Varieties of Religious Experience*, Penguin, 1983

Jamie, Kathleen, *Findings*, Sort of Books, 2005

Jenkins, Alan, *The Book of the Thames*, Macmillan, 1983

Kant, Immanuel, *Critique of Pure Reason*, Penguin, 2007

Karnazes, Dean, *Ultramarathon Man: Confessions of an All-night Runner*, Jeremy P. Tarcher, 2006

Koestler, Arthur, *The Act of Creation*, Arkana, 1989

Kozik, Frantisek and Zátopek, Emil, *Emil Zátopek in Photographs*, Aria, 1954

Krabbé, Tim, *The Rider*, Bloomsbury, 2002

Lydiard, Arthur, *Running with Lydiard*, Meyer & Meyer, 2001

Mabey, Richard, *Nature Cure*, Vintage, 2008

McConnell, Kym, *Extreme Running*, Pavilion, 2010

McDougall, Chris, *Born to Run: The Hidden Tribe, the Ultra-Runners, and the Greatest Race the World Has Never Seen*, Profile Books, 2010

MacFarlane, Robert, *Mountains of the Mind: A History of a Fascination*, Granta Books, 2008

——*The Wild Places*, Granta Books, 2008

Maitland, Sara, *A Book of Silence*, Granta Books, 2008

Mill, John Stuart, *Utilitarianism*, OUP, 1998

Murakami, Haruki, *What I Talk about When I Talk about Running*, Vintage, 2009

Nietzsche, Friedrich, *Ecce Homo: How One Becomes What One Is*, Penguin, 2004

Noakes, Tim, *Lore of Running*, Human Kinetics Europe Ltd, 2002

Perrottet, Tony, *The Naked Olympics: The True Story of the Olympic Games*, Random House USA, 2004

Petit, Philippe, *To Reach the Clouds*, Faber & Faber, 2008

Rackham, Oliver, *Woodlands*, HarperCollins, 2010

Radcliffe, Paula, *Paula: My Story So Far*, Pocket Books, 2005

Rambali, Paul, *Barefoot Runner: The Life of Marathon Champion Abebe Bikila*, Serpent's Tail, 2008

Rew, Kate, *Wild Swim*, Guardian Books, 2009

Rousseau, Jean-Jacques, *Reveries of the Solitary Walker*, Penguin, 2004

Saint-Exupéry, Antoine de, *Night Flight*, Penguin, 2000

——, *Wind, Sand and Stars*, Penguin, 2000

Scarry, Elaine, *The Body in Pain: The Making and Unmaking of the World*, OUP, 1988

Schama, Simon, *Landscape and Memory*, Harper Perennial, 2004

Schopenhauer, Arthur, *The World as Will and Representation*, Dover Publications, 1967

Sebald, W. G., *The Rings of Saturn*, Vintage, 2002

Sillitoe, Alan, *The Loneliness of the Long Distance Runner*, Harper Perennial, 2007

Smiles, Samuel, *Self-Help*, OUP, 2008

Solnit, Rebecca, *A Field Guide to Getting Lost*, Canongate Books Ltd, 2006

——, *Wanderlust: A History of Walking*, Verso, 2006

Spivey, Nigel, *The Ancient Olympics: War Minus the Shooting*, OUP, 2005

Sprawson, Charles, *Haunts of the Black Masseur: The Swimmer as Hero*, Vintage, 1993

Stroud, Mike, *Survival of the Fittest: Anatomy of Peak Physical Performance*, Yellow Jersey Press, 2004

Swale-Pope, Rosie, *Just a Little Run Around the World*, Harper True, 2009

Terray, Lionel, *Conquistadors of the Useless*, Baton Wicks Publications, 2000

Thoreau, Henry David, *Walden: Or, Life in the Woods*, Dover, 1995

——, *Walking*, Filiquarian Publishing, 2008

Wainwright, Alfred, *The Wainwright Memorial Walk*, Frances Lincoln, 2004

Welch, Denton, *A Voice Through a Cloud*, Enitharmon Press, 2004

——, *I Left My Grandfather's House*, Enitharmon Press, 2006

Wheeler, Sara, *Cherry: A Life of Apsley Cherry-Garrard*, Vintage, 2002

Wilson, E. O., *Biophilia*, Harvard University Press, 1990

Wright, Patrick, *The River: The Thames in Our Time*, BBC Books, 1999

Yates, Frances A., *The Art of Memory*, Pimlico, 1992

Zahab, Ray, *Running for My Life: On the Extreme Road with Adventure Runner Ray Zahab*, Insomniac Press, 2007

Running Websites

Athens Marathon	www.athensmarathon.com
Badwater Ultra	www.badwater.com
Bob Graham	www.bobgrahamclub.co.uk
London Marathon	www.virginlondonmarathon.com
Marathon des Sables	www.saharamarathon.co.uk
Mont Blanc Ultra	www.ultratrailmb.com
Paris Marathon	www.parismarathon.com
Picnic Marathon	www.trionium.com/picnic
Round Rotherham 50-mile Ultra	www.hmarston.co.uk/rhac/trail/rrr.htm
Runner's World	www.runnersworld.co.uk
Spartathlon	www.spartathlon.gr
Sri Chinmoy Self-transcendence	www.multidays.com
Ultra-distance calendar	www.ultramarathonrunning.com/races
Rory Coleman	www.rorycoleman.co.uk
Scott Jurek	www.scottjurek.com
Dean Karnazes	www.ultramarathonman.com
Yannis Kouros	www.yianniskouros.com
Chris McDougall	www.chrismcdougall.com
Rosie Swale-Pope	www.rosiearoundtheworld.co.uk

The author and publisher do not take responsibility for any of the content of external websites.